the SIMPLE act of READING

the SIMPLE act of READING

EDITED BY DEBRA ADELAIDE

Anita Heiss, Andy Griffiths, Fiona McFarlane, Giulia Giuffrè,
David Malouf, Joan London, Kate Forsyth, Geordie Williamson,
Rosie Scott, Tegan Bennett Daylight, Wayne Macauley, Jill Jones,
Gabrielle Carey, Sunil Badami, Catherine Keenan, Debra Adelaide,
Luke Davies, Carrie Tiffany, Gail Jones, Malcolm Knox and Delia Falconer

VINTAGE BOOKS
Australia

A Vintage book
Published by Random House Australia Pty Ltd
Level 3, 100 Pacific Highway, North Sydney NSW 2060
www.randomhouse.com.au

Penguin Random House
RANDOM HOUSE BOOKS

First published by Vintage in 2015

Random House Books is part of the Penguin Random House group of companies whose addresses can be found at global.penguinrandomhouse.com.

COPYRIGHT AGENCY CULTURAL FUND

Copyright Agency and its members are committed to supporting our creative industries and building a strong foundation for Australian creators.

National Library of Australia
Cataloguing-in-Publication entry

The simple act of reading/Debra Adelaide

ISBN 978 0 85798 624 5 (paperback)

Books and reading
Authors and readers
Other Creators/Contributors:
Adelaide, Debra, 1958– editor

028

Cover image © Trevillion Images
Cover design by Christabella Designs
Typeset in 11.5/15 pt Bembo by Midland Typesetters, Australia
Printed in Australia by Griffin Press, an accredited ISO AS/NZS 14001:2004 Environmental Management System printer

Random House Australia uses papers that are natural, renewable and recyclable products and made from wood grown in sustainable forests. The logging and manufacturing processes are expected to conform to the environmental regulations of the country of origin.

Writers on READING in support of THE SYDNEY STORY FACTORY

Contents

For it is in the simple act of reading where the living and the dead, the real and the imagined, meet. It is in the simple act of reading where we exercise those two most sacred of human vocations: compassion and creativity. For as we know, without either of these primes there is no possibility for a humanity present or past worth talking about.

Junot Díaz

Introduction

Debra Adelaide

I COULD NOT IMAGINE A MORE PERFECT BOOK THAN this: a collection of essays by writers I admire about the one thing that has preoccupied me my entire life.

The idea for this book was simple, as simple as the act of reading itself: how compelling it is when authors write about books, other authors or just moments in their reading lives that have been significant for them. I'd had my eye on several essays published in recent years, such as by Luke Davies and Carrie Tiffany, pieces that express what I love about how vital reading is: treasured childhood reading experiences, connections with particular authors or moments in life when reading in general, or just a particular book, represents a turning point.

I was lucky that these people agreed to have their work reappear in this collection, fortunate again in acquiring other similar contributions, from people like Tegan Bennett Daylight, Gail Jones and David Malouf, and then blessed again to gather a whole collection of new pieces by other contributors, among them Delia Falconer, Jill Jones, Fiona McFarlane and Geordie Williamson.

The brief was quite simple too: write about any aspect of the reading life that is meaningful to you, and will be to those interested in what makes writers tick. And because this book was compiled and published with the object of supporting young readers and writers via the work of the Sydney Story Factory, many authors concentrated on what and how they read in childhood or as young adults: Sunil Badami, Kate Forsyth, Andy Griffiths, Rosie Scott. And even why they might not once have read, or what it was like before they became readers, such as Catherine Keenan and Anita Heiss. As a special indulgence I was able to include pieces on particular authors and books of great significance: Wayne Macauley on Gerald Murnane's *The Plains*, and Joan London on Elizabeth Harrower's *The Watch Tower*.

Specific acts of reading are represented here, such as Gabrielle Carey on reading *Finnegans Wake* in collaboration, and Malcolm Knox on ereaders versus 'real' books; while the whole heady experience of the reading life is captured in Giulia Giuffrè's singular chapter on reading and secrets.

Reading connects us with our younger selves. Reading anything as an adult has the potential to shoot us back to the time when we were learning to read and angry that the letters wouldn't form into words, or were flooded with the joy and sense of accomplishment when they finally did. When we were closing the pages on our first real chapter book, reading without the aid of illustrations, or staying up late and waking early to finish that amazing story. Many of the authors here talk about the remembering – and the forgetting – involved with what they read as children, of the physical power of reading to summon up experiences from long ago and often repressed.

Science has in recent years proven what bookish types have always known intuitively: reading is good for you. Reading fiction is especially good for you, and reading literary fiction positively endows you with emotional and intellectual health. Empathy, sensitivity, perception and understanding of social nuance and complexity are all improved after an individual reads a story or novel. Researchers have even set short extracts from authors and then after a few minutes tested participants' abilities to interpret emotions and gauge people's thoughts, beliefs and expectations. The results show that skills in all these fields improve dramatically.

A few pages of Austen or Proust before addressing that stressful meeting. A cummings poem while priming yourself for a first date. A chapter or poem by either of the Eliots before confronting the neighbour about that barking dog. Maybe not *On the Road* before a driving test . . . but aside from that, the applications of good literature are almost endless.

Above all, what's clear from this collection is not necessarily what books we read, and continue to read, but how. How reading forges mysterious and vital pathways through our brains; how it fires up the imagination, leads us into endless divergent crisscrossing pathways through a veritable forest of literature; how it nurtures enquiry, curiosity and engagement with worlds outside of ourselves. How it dispels ignorance, makes dreams seem true, fosters sympathy. There's a list of books and authors at the end of this collection, compiled from all the titles that the contributors mention in their pieces, and it's amazing how diverse it is, and how some authors or books never go away despite the changes in political and cultural values over the years (Enid Blyton and C. S. Lewis scored pretty high here). Lowbrow or highbrow, the books on this list are a reminder that a reader truly is a consumer, ingesting the words in an almost physical way, hungry for anything and everything. Perhaps this is why the term *voracious* applies to readers, why in this collection writers use words like *glutton* or *devouring* to describe the experience: our appetite for books can never be sated.

There is a give and take in the physical reading experience. Several contributors comment on the physical activity, the body that recalls where it was when it read this or that book, the experience that is instantly relived when a book is picked up again after decades. And they talk about the opposite experience, of being taken away from themselves, from their bodies, as they are drawn into that other world within the book they are reading. They can tell you all about where they were the first time they read a certain novel, in which library collection they discovered one author or another, the most vivid details of that particular school term or summer holiday when they first read Jeffrey Archer or J. R. R. Tolkien or Charlotte Brontë. And they will also say they were reading as if in a dream, their entire selves transported to a whole new world.

Addressing the Sydney Writers' Festival in 2008, Junot Díaz declared, 'It is in the simple act of reading where we exercise those two most sacred of human vocations: compassion and creativity.' These are some of the most important qualities we hope to nurture in young readers, in our own children if we have them, in our students if we are teachers, and in the readers of our own work, the generations that will follow in our steps. This is why the work of the Sydney Story Factory is so important, encouraging young writers who must of course also be readers in that symbiotic way, and why we're so glad to be able to produce this book.

Find a quiet place, open the page, follow the line of words: the act of reading might be simple but as these splendid essays demonstrate, it is also one of the most important things in all this human world.

'The Tintin *books were my emotional universe. To read them felt quite simply like being loved: in advance, and by an entire world of pure possibility, my future.'*

Luke Davies

Hergé and Me

Luke Davies

MY FATHER REMEMBERS THE MOMENT, SOME TIME early in 1971. Nine years old, I casually announced to him that I planned to write to *Tintin* author Hergé, and that I needed his help in finding an address. 'You predicted to me how things would play out,' my father tells me, when I call him as I prepare to write this story. 'You said you'd write back and forth and tell each other what was going on. You were relaxed and happy about it. I tried to gently pour cold water on the idea – I told you that thousands of kids probably wrote to him, and that he mightn't have time to get back to you individually. But you shrugged it off.'

Dad tracked down the address for Methuen Publishers in London, and away I wrote. To my father's surprise and my own joy, a couple of months later a beautiful letter turned up. An embossed Tintin waved to me from the envelope, his faithful dog Snowy trotting happily alongside him.

'Dear Luke,' the letter began. 'It was a very kind and interesting letter you sent me, and I thank you very much for writing it.'

My heart leapt. I do not now, over forty years later, remember that casual confidence with which I had sent my father on his address-finding expedition; but I do remember the intake of breath, the sudden sense of my world expanding, when I opened that letter.

For the *Tintin* books were my emotional universe. To read them felt quite simply like being loved: in advance, and by an entire world of pure possibility, my future. But to write to the author was to reach out for the lover. Even today, the power of reading one remains visceral: each book acts as a form of transportation, not just to the emotional landscape of this first literary love affair, but to very specific memories.

One summer morning the family began the trek up the Pacific Highway from home in Sydney to Surfers Paradise, where each year we spent our Christmas holidays. The usual twelve-hour highway dash was interrupted when my little brother, Felix, who'd had an ongoing illness since birth, got sick halfway through the journey and wound up having to spend the night in Grafton Base Hospital. We booked into an old-fashioned pub by the Clarence River. The situation with Felix mustn't have been great, because there was about an hour around dusk when our parents left me and my older brother, Ben, on our own in the hotel room. I remember feeling: 'Okay. We're alone in an alien place and our parents aren't here. When they come back, they'll feed us.' I curled up on my lumpy bed with *Prisoners of the Sun* and dived, transported, into its noir-ish, scene-setting opening panel: 'At Police Headquarters in Callao, Peru.'

Even now as I write four decades later, I remember everything about that hotel room: the stripe of the bed cover, the great cedar cupboard, the gauze curtains, the alkaline breeze from the river. And with it all I remember so vividly the unassailable cosiness, the sense of protectedness, being in such an utterly foreign room and yet being, with that book in my hands, fundamentally safe. Certain books in my life have seemed psychically talismanic, but only *Tintin* books ever felt *physically* so.

From time to time it has struck me that as a writer I've somehow managed to live my life as I had long ago dreamt of doing, based on the Tintin paradigm: on my toes, travelling, senses attenuated, everything just adventure and exploration, curiosity and problem-solving. There's a frame in one of the books where Tintin is sitting in his cosy apartment having a boiled egg and toast for breakfast, reading the newspaper. In European cities, when I've sometimes rented some apartment to work on a novel or script, I have found myself thinking, in the middle of such a breakfast, and with a conscious, overt memory of that scene: 'Holy shit – I think I've pulled this off.' At such a moment one is infused with gratitude: that life, for all the unfathomable strangeness of its twists and turns, can now and again integrate, without static, the joys and dreams of the deep past with the radiant present.

We wrote several letters back and forth over the next few years. Perhaps I'll never know if it was him composing them or some secretary – were there really thousands of children writing to him? – but there was a remarkable consistency to his tone and style across the letters, so I'll choose to believe it was him, if not physically operating the typewriter then at least dictating them.

'I wish I could come and jump in your Moon Balloon,' he wrote – referring to I have no idea what – 'but this year it is impossible: I'm flying next week to Thailand and Taiwan.' 'I was especially delighted by your father's big idea of "The Butterfly Farm",' he wrote, in another letter. 'Respect for and interest in life are always a comforting show.' I must have bombarded him with questions. 'I am married but have no children,' he answered in one letter, 'except, of course, Tintin, Captain Haddock, Professor Calculus and all the others, and that's a family!'

There were elaborate Christmas cards, too. One, a frosted gold scene of Tintin and the others going to church in the snow, opened up into a spiral that hung from the ceiling. Others showed various characters, disguised on an Egyptian tomb mural, or as figures on a sheet of stamps, or a crowd of protestors saying 'Non!' to pollution.

One is even a full-page rough in progress from *Tintin and the Picaros*, Hergé's final book, complete with a *trompe l'oeil* 'best wishes' card attached with a 'fake' rusty paperclip.

Then it seems – to my great regret now – that with adolescence coming on, I simply stopped writing. And so did he. But every year for seven years the Christmas cards kept coming: extravagant, beautiful, playful. And what of my side of the correspondence? Another thought struck me as I prepared to write this story: surely copies of my original letters to Hergé would not still exist? I wrote, without an enormous amount of hope, to the Hergé Foundation. The archivist, Bernard Tordeur, replied. He told me that there were 50,000 letters in storage in a 'safe place somewhere out of Brussels', and that while they weren't digitised, he would at some point try to see if he could find mine. (Tordeur also confirmed to me that 'Hergé wrote his own letters, [which] were [then] typed by a secretary.')

My heart leapt all over again. I experienced even my mounting impatience as an intense sensation of good fortune. I was to get to see the way I thought, the way I wrote, more than forty years ago. Primary sources! Eventually Tordeur unearthed three artefacts only: nothing from those first couple of years, and unfortunately not the first letter I ever wrote Hergé at nine, which I craved as a kind of Holy Grail. But a priceless, personal goldmine nonetheless.

There's a letter from 1973, in which I appear to be doing exactly what I told my father I'd do: chit-chat. 'For our holiday we went down to Sydney and went to various tourist attractions, picture theatres, ferry-rides etc.,' I wrote. '[M]um and I went into a bookshop to buy a Tintin book for me, which is *Red Rackham's Treasure*. That now brings my collection to six of your books.' 'Ben, who is twelve, is learning French like most other Australian 1st formers, [and] is going to collect all your books that are in French when he gets better at the language.' (Historical note: he never got better; no such collection exists.)

There's one other letter, from a year and a half later; I was a few months short of my thirteenth birthday by now. 'Dear Mr Hergé,

I hope you are well. I'm sorry I haven't written to you for so long. I wrote one letter to you recently, but it must have got lost in the mail, as I never heard back from you.' To the modern ear, in this era of chronic, overwhelming, undealt-with email inboxes, there sounds a hint of the passive-aggressive in this. But it speaks to me of my innocence: I simply assumed only one possible explanation – lost in the mail – for any downturn in correspondence.

'Next year,' I wrote, 'in 2nd form, I have chosen for my two elective subjects French and Latin. Maybe I'll soon be writing to you in French.' (Historical note: I never wrote to him in either language.)

Monsieur Tordeur's third treasure is a school photo of me in my St Dominic's College, Penrith uniform – a school I only attended for a year and a term, and a photo of which I have no memory. Hergé had sent me a photo of himself, signed in gold ink, for my eleventh birthday. I suppose this was the reciprocal act. 'Dear Mr Hergé,' I inscribed, on the back of the photo, 'With great affection, from Luke Davies (aged 11) (Australia)'.

'You were relaxed and happy about it,' my father had said, and I'm amazed, looking through this window into the past, by just how unfazed I do seem to have been by it all, how *not* in awe of this man whose work I worshipped so. 'With great affection,' indeed. For darker times would come when I was not at all relaxed – an era I would explore in my novel *Candy*. And the fact that I still have the cards and letters – indeed, the very existence of this article – is closely related to an extraordinary sequence of events that occurred much later.

When I was nineteen or twenty, studying Arts at Sydney University, I knew a couple of the editors of *Honi Soit*, the student newspaper. A young cartoonist, David Messer, was fooling around with *Tintin* mash-ups on the back page – taking strips from the existing books (I daresay illegally) and morphing some of the dialogue and pictures, making Tintin not just a young adventurer but seemingly an adventurer-cum-drug-addled rogue as well. At some point, liking what he was doing, I must have lent him the cards and letters.

And promptly thought no more of the loan. Extraordinary though this seems to me now, I remember only that I was heading towards the precipice over which would lie a tumbling into years of chaos.

Jump forward seven or eight dark, demented years, and life had finally collapsed into the heap it was always going to collapse into. I was discharged from the Langton Centre, a detox facility in Surry Hills, and told I had to wait three days for a bed to become available in the rehab into which I'd been accepted. The catch was, you could only enter the rehab directly from the Centre. They said they'd make an exception for me, but only if I stayed at the house of someone who was in recovery. (I knew very few such people.) Through a friend of a friend, I found a sofa I could crash on for the weekend – at the house of a woman, a few years clean, who had a twelve-year-old daughter and a three-year-old son.

I was three weeks off drugs for the first time in near a decade. Life seemed hallucinatory, raw, bewildering. Mostly what I remember is craving milk. Everything was about to change, and I had absolutely no idea what that meant or what it would feel like. There were a few *Tintin* books in the bookshelves in the living room. 'I was so into him as a kid,' I said. 'You know, I even wrote to the author and he sent me all these letters and cards.'

My host replied, 'Oh wow, you should see what *we've* got.' She took me to her daughter's room and pulled out a filing box. And there – unthought-of for eight years – was my Hergé trove. After the first moment of incomprehensibility, after my jaw dropped, after the flush of goosebumps – after I almost fell to my knees – I stammered, 'These . . . these are mine. You found my letters!'

She thought I was joking; why would you not? 'Look,' I pointed to the envelopes: every one of them addressed to Luke Davies. 'Where did you get these?'

What had happened was, a couple of years after I'd given the packet to David Messer the cartoonist, a new *Honi Soit* editor had been clearing out old junk from the newspaper offices, and had come across the cards. He thought they were an interesting curio, and held on to them. As it turned out, this fellow was a friend of the woman I stayed with that fateful weekend, and at some point, when her daughter was eight or nine, he'd noticed that she liked *Tintin*, and had given her my cards and letters as a gift.

It was all so improbable, so exhilarating, the letters' journey through the years and back full circle to me. The odds against the rehab not having a bed immediately available; my having to camp out at a stranger's house; the fact that deep in the stranger's house, like an amulet in some fairytale, would be my long-lost letters; the fact I even noticed a stray *Tintin* book in a bookshelf. It is as if at that moment my old life – that innocent boy – was being given back to me, in the form of a new life; and everything in-between was wiped clean-slate. (Historical fact: it wasn't, technically speaking. Oh, the wreckage. Oh, the clean-up operation.) What was extraordinary was not even that the letters still existed, but that, against all odds, they had found their way back to me. If I'd never been at that house that weekend, I think years later I might have idly thought: 'What the *hell* ever happened to those Hergé letters?' Instead, I get to keep the amulet.

Maurice Sendak, author of *Where the Wild Things Are*, once related the following anecdote. 'A little boy sent me a charming card with a little drawing on it. I loved it. I answer all my children's letters – sometimes very hastily – but this one I lingered over. I sent him a card and I drew a picture of a Wild Thing on it. I wrote, "Dear Jim: I loved your card." Then I got a letter back from his mother and she said, "Jim loved your card so much he ate it." That to me was one of the highest compliments I've ever received. He didn't care that it was an original Maurice Sendak drawing or anything. He saw it, he loved it, he ate it.'

I relate to that little boy's ritualistic, proto-religious ingestion, his desire for total communion with the Other, for that which has given him joy. It's a magnificent moment in obsessive fandom.

But I'm very glad that by nine years old I had a more sophisticated sense of what to eat, and what to leave alone.

'I loved taking out the plain, severe little copies of the classics with their delicate typeface, tissue-thin pages, musty smell, the worlds within. I absorbed by osmosis their rather stern precepts, which made absolute sense to me at the time.'

ROSIE SCOTT

Reading for Life

Rosie Scott

IF THERE WAS AN EQUIVALENT OF A BIBLE IN OUR socialist household, it was *The Family of Man*, Edward Steichen's classic book of photography and writings for the Museum of Modern Art. As a very young child I pored over it so many times the words and images fused forever in my mind. Steichen's kind face behind his rimless glasses, the eyes of the woman gnawing at a scrap of bread, a Jamaican's face swollen with love as he cradled his son in the curve of his arm: each picture was in itself a little world, a story that I stared at, endlessly fascinated. I saw that it could reveal the perplexing secrets of the adult world if I puzzled over it long enough. Instinctively I trusted its truthfulness, the sober love with which it was put together, its calm assumption of the triumph of good. It was there in all its rich unsentimentality, the life of adults; men and women toiling, grieving and laughing, the quarrels and exuberance of love, the beauty of the unknown and the comfort of the known.

The captions were to me even more powerful than the pictures. *The Family of Man* was the book that first showed me the real power of words to stir people to action: William Blake, Shakespeare, Thomas Paine, the bible, Plato, Anne Frank, Georges Sand, *The Bhagavad Gita*, Carl Sandburg were all represented. The quotes I read there inspired me to read more; they were a taste of a spectacular world of poetic eloquence:

> 'The little ones leaped, and shouted, and laugh'd
> And all the hills echoed . . .'
>
> 'But such is the irresistible nature of truth, that all it asks, and all it wants, is the liberty of appearing.'
>
> 'For Mercy has a human heart,
> Pity a human face . . .'
>
> 'I still believe people are really good at heart.'
>
> 'I know of no safe depository of the ultimate powers of society but the people themselves.'
>
> 'Humanity is outraged in me and with me. We must not dissimulate nor try to forget this indignation which is one of the most passionate forms of love.'
>
> 'Who is on my side? Who?'
>
> 'The land is a mother that never dies.'

The Diary of Anne Frank was given to me for my eleventh birthday and it had an electric effect. I too kept a diary; I too believed my mother loved my older sister best. It was Anne's truthfulness that instantly impressed me, the unassuming clarity of her vision. I loved her like a sister and read the book over and over again, crying every time I reached the epilogue: 'She died in Bergen-Belsen with the same qualities of courage and endurance which had already made her noteworthy in Auschwitz.' Anne taught me that, provided it is absolutely truthful, a diary was a means of making sense of your life. She analysed herself and the people around her with humility, humour and a formidable intelligence. Her courage shone from every page. Like all true heroines she gave me hope and faith in the possibilities of the human spirit and taught me the enduring power of literature to speak the truth.

At the same time I was trying my hand with my own writing, experimenting all the time, and each story I wrote from ten years old onwards reflected the writer I was currently reading. There are crude traces of the styles of Edgar Allen Poe, Dickens, Jane Austen, L. M. Montgomery, Salinger, and Anne Frank among others, but slowly and shakily I began to develop my own voice.

When I was twelve our family moved from Sandringham in Auckland to Titirangi, a leafy suburb in the foothills of the Waitakeres, scene of the wild west-coast setting of Jane Campion's famous movie *The Piano*. Titirangi means fringe of heaven in Maori, and after the drab, treeless, genteel suburb we'd just left, this community of writers, artists and bohemians was certainly glorious. We were like wide-eyed innocents catapulted straight into paradise.

My father for one took to our new life as if he'd been born to it. Startling new worlds were opening up, the rigid mentality of New Zealand in the 1950s cracking open at last. My parents had left the Orwellian absurdities of the New Zealand Communist Party and Sandringham gentility in one fell swoop to dive head first into an upper-middle-class, fast-track, decadent, bohemian world. The moderating boundaries of suburban life, bringing up young children, all the safe nose-to-the-grindstone routine, suddenly went up in flames.

Those early years in Titirangi were so full of promise and drama that they gave me a sense of limitless possibilities and with them, almost constant anxiety. It was both sophisticated and nerve-wracking for me in a way that nothing ever was again. Salinger was the writer who epitomised the era for me: coldly elegant, brilliant, neurotic, women-hating and deeply seductive.

Like all precocious young readers of the very early 1960s, I was struck by *Catcher in the Rye*'s revelations about the coolness of alienation and the phoniness of the world. It was our own most secret voice, alluring and wonderful, and I devoured all of Salinger's books. I wrote a book review for school in which I recklessly tried to compare *Franny and Zooey* to *Pride and Prejudice*.

It was the first time I'd read a writer who was familiar with people so similar to my own family. It was only many years later that, even though I still loved the book, I understood why John Lennon's killer had a copy in his pocket when he shot Lennon. Or what an anti-woman rave *Franny and Zooey* is, as Zooey slowly cuts the ground from under Franny's feet with every word, denying her reality and identity with that subtle technique most women become pretty familiar with at some time in their lives.

One of the many anxieties of my life at that time was about sex. Though I was deeply interested in it, I was still very ambivalent, partly because of the rampant contempt of women so endemic then. Many of the middle-aged men in those unreconstructed days were not above making passes at us very young girls. One accused me of being frigid at the age of fourteen when I rebuffed him – all of which alarmed and confused me. In his soaring classic *On the Road*, which I read with great excitement and loved for its passionate anarchy, Kerouac wrote:

> Out on the dawn streets, Dean said, 'Now you see, man, there's *real* woman for you. Never a harsh word, never a complaint, or modified; her old man can come in any hour of the night with anybody and have talks in the kitchen and drink the beer and leave any old time. This is a man, that's his castle.'

That was our understanding of what it was to be a woman, that kind of gentle, persuasive, bohemian portrait of women's real significance in the world.

Nearer to home, terrifying in its vindictiveness and proof of Germaine Greer's comment about how much some men hate women, was the poem I read by James K. Baxter, a great New Zealand poet:

Sam Hunt, Sam Hunt, Sam Hunt, Sam Hunt
The housewife with her oyster cunt
Has pissed upon what might have been
Lively, original and green . . .
The Pill, the Rags, the Summer Sale
Put Venus and her tribe in jail
Till every fuck's a coffin-nail . . .

Sam Hunt is another of New Zealand's most famous poets. He once wrote a poem dedicated to me and described a black raven between my thighs which I never quite understood – but it was certainly an improvement on the oyster.

There was something in my father's make-up that accepted this attitude towards women, the need for a woman to be aglow with the joy of giving away her life gracefully for her man. I saw through his eyes his beautiful, giggly, slightly submissive girlfriend who never made a fuss and hung on men's words, and my mother's strong lined face, unmade-up, her bitterness over his treatment of her.

We were brought up with this message; it was bred in our bones. Even our mother herself sometimes subscribed to it in her advice to us in those pre-feminist times. Once again it was life-changing books like Betty Friedan's *The Feminine Mystique* and much later *The Women's Room* by Marilyn French (who afterwards became a close friend) that caused me to see it was a message for slaves. We had internalised this message to such a degree that we felt it was somehow ugly and unfeminine and graceless if we did not give way to men's wishes.

It took time and energy and marvellous books like these to see sexism for what it was.

I was twelve going on thirty, apprehensive but fascinated, meeting the kind of people I had never known existed, roaming the Titirangi bush, going to coffee bars and parties, listening to conversations that enthralled me. It was a world of innocence and extreme cynicism, of wit, of being on your mettle intellectually, and, among the adults I knew, a world of sexual adventuring, heavy drinking, and an unselfconscious women-hating, which I registered but still had no words for; a masculinist brittle intellectualism that was heady and exciting. There was a kind of crackling promise in the air which I have never experienced since.

My father was at the time on the way to becoming a well-known historian after a slow beginning. His most impressive subject was Te Whiti O Rongomai, Maori prophet and leader, visionary, a man of great subtlety, eloquence and political genius. Years ago as a young man, my father had visited a small neglected marae and talked to some old kuia there. It was in this way that he had found out about the extraordinary prophet, who organised his people in effective Gandhi-like protests – long before Gandhi – against the land grab by Europeans. There is a photo of my father, looking uncannily like a boyish Woody Allen, standing on Te Whiti's marae with the awed, disbelieving look of someone who has just stumbled into history heaven.

The book he wrote about Te Whiti, called *A Parihaka Story* and later, in a new edition, *Ask That Mountain*, was years on voted one of the ten most influential books in New Zealand and has had nine editions. Because my father didn't have a history degree, he was at first treated with scorn by many of New Zealand's established historians, but he has since been showered with honours. It was his interest as a historian and teacher of his children to pay tribute to unsung heroes and heroines whose acts of courage or altruism stood out. If history is written by the oppressors, his mission was to shake the balance out by telling the stories that illustrated the possibility of rationality, moral sense and a kind of tenderness in the management of human affairs.

So we were a very bookish family, and once we three sisters started blossoming, there was a constant stream of suitors to the house, including many writers, most of whom were wildly unsuitable. There was also a racy undercurrent: all the adults we knew seemed to be having affairs. My father was one of them – he fell in love with a beautiful American woman, wife of a visiting psychology professor. This caused my mother endless grief and hurt and in the end was a catalyst for the break-up of their marriage. We children were always aware of these dramas, so things were pretty chaotic at home.

Looking back on that exciting, confusing period in my life, I realise the books I was reading at the time gave me a kind of moral compass, a guide to coping with the adults in my life and a way of shoring up my precarious identity. I read Steinbeck, Dos Passos, Agee and Fast as well as New Zealand writers like John Mulgan, Janet Frame, Katherine Mansfield and Ronald Morrieson. Every week I read one modern novel from the library and one classic, working my way through the joys of Zola, Hugo and Eliot, and the first of many re-readings of Austen and Dickens. The Russian classics, which I also loved, came a little later, as did all those weird macho kings of the early 1960s like Miller, Mailer and John Rechy with their louche, outrageous misogyny. At that suggestible age every book was a discovery and serious obligation. Once I chose one I felt duty-bound to finish it, however much it dragged.

I used to walk along the green tunnel of Rangiwai Crescent to the library, which was hushed and lovely, with views of the sea and bush from every window, and even that walk up our soft country road was a joy in itself. I loved taking out the plain, severe little copies of the classics with their delicate typeface, tissue-thin pages, musty smell, the worlds within. I absorbed by osmosis their rather stern precepts, which made absolute sense to me at the time. The simple but potent message I took from them as a young girl was that there was such a thing as moral courage, and that with the help of this admirable quality the most intractable problems could be overcome.

Jane Austen, for instance, in her austere, superbly witty, insightful way, seemed to me to prove conclusively by her stories and characterisation that common sense, kindness and a strong sense of self would always prevail over the lies, trickiness and downright evil of characters such as John Willoughby. People like him, whom I recognised in my own life, were all so charming, powerful and plausible and so seemingly untouchable that it seemed inevitable they would win over the flawed, powerless heroines. I liked the fact that hers was not a black and white, romantic view of life, that she was writing about recognisable people and the kind of dilemmas I was facing in my own family. She convinced me that though troubles can seem to be never-ending and push you to unimaginable limits, in the end constancy, truthfulness, courage, patience and kindness can win out. The astuteness of her writerly voice was a kindly if rather acerbic guide for me.

Dickens appealed in a slightly different way. His books showed social injustice was something that could be challenged and changed. His much more robust depiction of evil, his deliciously satiric view of human behaviour, his social engagement and labyrinthine plots absolutely enthralled me. As with my reading of Austen, I felt the security and sense of his underlying values: that though wickedness flourishes and seems all-powerful, it can crumble away under the steady application of courage, humour and steadfastness.

Most adolescents believe, as I did, that their troubles are unique to them and will never end. Cultural rituals that celebrate the attaining of adulthood and the adolescent's own burgeoning maturity teach otherwise. In my case, reading was my main teacher. Throughout my childhood and adolescence, reading, like writing, was always there – a parallel, private universe; a constant. As soon as I learnt to read, I began my lifelong habit of reading continuously and at great speed, ravenous as a junkie, never tiring of it. It was essential both as an escape and an engagement with the world. It put into words my fledgling political ideas and passions. It gave me that moral compass. It was also a constant exposure to all the technical possibilities and parameters of style; it gave me an understanding of what I could do as a writer, the sure knowledge that almost anything was possible.

Above all, in a similar process to writing, it was the creation of another place in my head, the feeling of sinking into it, lost and absorbed, the real world outside suspended at least for a few hours. And that is still one of my greatest pleasures.

'A great book is a companion, a friend, and like a friend, it changes with you.'

TEGAN BENNETT DAYLIGHT

A Phone Call to Helen Garner

Tegan Bennett Daylight

HOLDEN CAULFIELD SAYS, 'WHAT REALLY KNOCKS ME out is a book that, when you're all done reading it, you wish the author that wrote it was a terrific friend of yours and you could call him up on the phone whenever you felt like it.' All great writing does this; seems to demand a reply, a response of some kind. Each time a writer writes they are making that phone call, to all of the writers whose work they have read. This is my phone call to Helen Garner.

I first encountered Garner's work in my teens, when I found a copy of *Monkey Grip* on my parents' bookshelves. *Monkey Grip* is Garner's first in a list of closely autobiographical fiction and non-fiction. It tells the story of Nora and Javo. Nora is a woman in her thirties who is living in a succession of shared households in inner-city Melbourne with her young daughter, Grace. Her life has a constantly changing shape. She has no single job (rather a succession of hazy freelance writing jobs) nor anywhere she must be. She shares the care of Grace with other mothers – and, occasionally, fathers – with whom she lives. She takes drugs. She has sex with many different men, but she is finally and hopelessly in love with Javo, another middle-class white Australian, but this time a junkie. His addiction spells disaster for their attachment, though disaster never quite, or never completely, arrives.

Monkey Grip keeps us in the same limbo experienced by its narrator. Just when we think we have seen the last of Javo, he appears again. He comes to tell Nora that he loves her or that he doesn't; he comes to borrow money for drugs, or to swear that he will never use drugs again. He surges and recedes, surges and recedes.

I hadn't read such unstructured fiction before – the crashing of the waves of junkie narrative made me feel sick and disoriented. But *Monkey Grip* changed reading for me. It was more than just the feeling of recognition that started my lifelong engagement with the work of Helen Garner, although recognition is the key to pleasure in literature. (The sense that one was just about to think what is on the page – the sense that that thought was only waiting for the writer to express it for us; this is why we read.) But reading Garner offered me more than recognition. For the first time I was consciously learning about *writing*. For the first time I was not reading for story (every so often I take up *Monkey Grip* to remind myself what happens in the 'end': Javo is a junkie; he continues to be a junkie; Nora continues to exist), but for words. I could see the work. I could see the writing.

I re-read it immediately. This time, I read it more slowly, not feeling so ill, unmoored in the sea of the story. It was so unusual in its form, so intimate in its expression, that I needed to know how it was written. I looked again and again at Garner's images, the way she saw things.

This scene comes from the early pages of *Monkey Grip*:

> We slept too lightly for rest. Early in the morning I climbed over him from the wall side of the bed, pulled my clothes on over my bloody legs, and wheeled my bike out his front door. A wild yellow sky, dry grey air full of turbulence. The street surfaces were burnished, blown clean as a bone. My bike tyres, pumped up hard, whirred on the glossy bitumen. Autumn, air, air, moving in dry warm blusters.

When I was younger these images altered the way I saw the world. They made me feel somehow present, alert to the shifts in light or weather, to the look of a street or a park or a house. A writer must be awake, and it was Garner who made me see this. She looked around her with an eye like a torch, sweeping across everything, selecting and rejecting, illuminating.

A great book is a companion, a friend, and like a friend, it changes with you. When I was a teenager, *Monkey Grip* did not speak directly to my own experience – in fact, it taught me about life, gave me some idea of what was to come. But when I re-read it, as I do most years, it makes me consider the life I am living now, with its similarities to Nora's (I have a daughter, lived for a long time in shared houses, and am also a writer) and its great differences (I live with my partner and two children and my experience with drugs and the miseries and pleasures of love affairs is a thing of the past). This passage, worth as much to me now as it was then, but changed now that I have changed myself, makes me consider how few of the day's deserted, illicit hours I currently inhabit. My life is more limited, more conventional than Nora's was. If I am out at night or very early in the morning, it is unusual. If I am, I will look at the sky and note how many stars there are or the quality of the new light. I will also notice how many people there are outside, pursuing their lives, when I seem to be always indoors. This is reading, waking you up, reminding you of how you live: Garner's writing, speaking to me now more than twenty-five years after my first engagement with it, makes me remember my teens and twenties and treasure them, for all those empty hours, for the warm air full of turbulence and the street surfaces blown clean as a bone.

Since then, I have read every word that Helen Garner has published, and most of them so many times that her syntax seems entwined with my DNA. Somewhere in one of Garner's early books, a girl holds a hose, and 'whacks' the 'silvery rope' of water against a window. It is not possible for me to see a running hose without thinking of this moment. When I write sometimes Garner's sentences surface in my mind; I feel myself imitating a certain rhythm she has. I know I am not the only Australian writer who experiences this. Her language is embedded in my way of thinking, and in the way of thinking of many readers. We would be different people without her.

Monkey Grip was published in 1977. It was met with some confusion and hostility by Australian reviewers, many of whom have lived to see their comments become part of the story of Garner's success (and the controversy she continues to stir up). The controversy centred, not just on the fact that Garner was writing explicitly about sex and women's desire, but that she had based her 'novel' on her diaries. Had she simply copied out her diaries, rather than written a novel in the 'right' way? This was hotly debated at the time. There was no question that Garner had done something to the novel, had dismantled our idea of what it should be, what a structure was, what a beginning, middle and end should be.

Years later, Garner defended herself against this criticism in her famous article 'I', published in the journal *Meanjin*:

> Shouldn't a real writer be writing about something other than herself and her immediate circle? I've been haunted by this question since 1977 when a reviewer of *Monkey Grip* asked irritably what the fuss was about: as far as he could see, all I'd done was publish my diaries. I went round for years after that in a lather of defensiveness: 'it's a novel, thank you very much'. But I'm too old to bother with that crap any more. I might as well come clean. I did publish my diary. That's exactly what I did. I left out what I thought were the boring bits, wrote bridging passages, and changed all the names.

Certainly *Monkey Grip* reads like a diary, with its return and return to the same beginning, its characters repeating themselves in patterns of love, difficulty, disappointment, love, difficulty, disappointment. Is it a novel? The same question has been asked about her latest piece of fiction, *The Spare Room*. It is a question worth asking, and worth examining. Let me simply say that *Monkey Grip* was, for me, a new kind of novel; not just a random accretion of information, but a thoughtfully observed, deeply felt work of art about a woman who has been caught, as Garner puts it, in 'the gap between theory and practice'. The book is not just about loving a junkie, it is about trying to love and let go at the same time; trying to put into practice the idea of 'free love', of shared partners; and trying to be stoic about the kind of pain this causes. For me, at least, Garner had cracked narrative open. She had written, in a way, the kind of fiction that Virginia Woolf had aspired to in novels like *To the Lighthouse*, and actually achieved in her own diaries. She had followed a consciousness that did not bend easily into the more traditional shape of a novel. She had written a women's novel.

If you read Helen Garner you will understand that she, too, is replying to the authors she has loved. The physical evidence is there – in her stories you will find books on every surface, read by children, read by adults, used as proof, as pleasure, as the source of argument. Her characters quote poetry and great prose. A description of a photograph of Tennyson opens *The Children's Bach*. In *The Spare Room* Helen and Nicola lie on their beds all afternoon 'reading mighty works of literature, shouting to each other analytical or admiring remarks'. This conversation between readers and writers reaches back over the centuries; it is going on still.

Helen Garner is the author of four novels, two novellas, a collection of short stories and five books of non-fiction, all of which are in print. Martin Amis says, 'When we say we love a writer's work, we are always stretching the truth: what we really mean is that we love about half of it. Sometimes rather more than half, sometimes rather less.' I love more than half of Garner's work. It is necessary, always, to read her closely, engaging with every sentence. Her writing, though never less than deeply political, is about detail. It does not lecture or harass, or try to curry favour. Garner looks around her and shows us what she sees. Her attention to the texture of life, to the silvery rope, to the 'juicy cough' of a granddaughter in *The Spare Room*, and to something as simple and as central as the weather, keeps us intent, absorbed, on every page. In *The Children's Bach*, spring comes, and 'in the morning, when the first person opened the back door, the whole bulk of air in the house shifted and warmed'.

It is spring as I write this. My experience of it will always be enhanced, expanded by the literature I read. Spring does not belong only to the young; because of writers like Garner, it also belongs to the reader.

'When I read, the real world disappears and only the invented world of the book remains. It is like stepping through a gateway into another time or another world, like slipping inside someone else's skin.'

KATE FORSYTH

Books Are Dangerous

Kate Forsyth

BOOKS ARE DANGEROUS.

I have known this ever since I set my bed on fire when I was about four years old. My sister and I had been tucked up, but I wanted to keep on reading. I waited until my mother had gone, and then I created a tent under my bedspread and dragged my bedside lamp inside, the light burning down on the page. Gradually my eyelids sank lower. Gradually my breathing deepened. I fell asleep (it must have been a really boring book to put me to sleep so fast). The paper began to smoulder. Smoke wreathed up. The book burst into flame. So did my bedspread. My mother has no sense of smell. Luckily for me, a friend had dropped by and mentioned the smell of burning. My mother rushed to check on my sleeping sister and me, and so was in time to save our lives.

When I tell school students this anecdote, I ask them, 'What do you think is the moral of this story?' Some good, obedient child always says, 'Don't read under the bedspread when you're meant to be asleep?'

'No!' I cry. 'I would never say "Don't read." The moral of the story is: *never read a boring book.* Read something that'll keep you up all night! Read one of my books (but make sure you use a torch, not a lamp)!' And being obedient children, they do.

I don't remember learning to read. It seemed to happen very easily and naturally. I do remember my first day at school. When my teacher realised I could read fluently, I got to spend the day sitting in a beanbag in a corner of the room with some books from the classroom library, while the other students were taught their ABCs. I went home in an absolute fever of delight and told my mother, 'I *love* school.' She was called in to speak to the principal and castigated for teaching me to read. My mother asked, 'How was I meant to stop her?'

The first novel I ever read by myself was *The Lion, the Witch and the Wardrobe* by C. S. Lewis. My sister, Belinda, and I were staying with our aunt, and she was reading it to us every night. Belinda and I were utterly enchanted by the story, and played Narnia games all day long. One day my sister aggravated me beyond endurance by reading on in the story, saying, 'You'll never believe what happens next!' I had to find out. As soon as she put the book down, I picked it up and began to puzzle my way through. Slowly the black hedge of thorns on the page parted, revealing a snowy landscape of dark trees through which the light of a lamp-post glowed . . .

It all begins with our eyes. Only the centre of our retina has enough resolution to recognise small print. It can see only one word or so at a time. Each word is split up into letters, syllables, prefixes, suffixes, phonemes. It must be put back together before our brain can recognise it as a word.

The neural networks of our brain then get to work. The phonological route located in the temporal lobe converts letters into speech sounds. The lexical route located in the frontal lobe gives meaning to the word. The limbic system deals with the emotional connotation of words, while the angular and supramarginal gyrus serve to link together the different parts of the brain . . . And all in less than one-fifth of a second.

Let's say it a little more simply. When we read the word 'cat', our brain sees those black marks on a white page, and at once sets to work to understand it. Our auditory processors give us the sound of the word so that we 'hear' it silently: *kuh* aaah tuh. Our temporal lobes give the word meaning: a small, furry, carnivorous mammal. Our visual processors create a mental image, which will be different for each individual and shaped by their own life experiences (I always see a black slinky creature with glowing green eyes and a hooked tail, but others may see a purring grey tabby or a fat orange tom). Our sensory processes remind us of the touch of a cat's silky fur, while our limbic system will imbue the word with emotional meaning. For some, delight. For others, disgust.

All this happens in a flash, our brains lighting up like globes of white fire. Meanwhile, our brain is sending out all kinds of signals that spark chemical responses in our bodies – the release of adrenaline if we're reading a thriller, oxytocin if we're reading a tear-jerker. Such chemical reactions can alter our brain's fundamental structure . . . forever.

No wonder books are so dangerous.

In the novel I am now writing, my heroine, Ava, is a young woman living in Berlin during the time of the Third Reich. On 10 May 1933 in Berlin, more than twenty-thousand books were burnt by the Nazis. Books by authors such as Sigmund Freud, Albert Einstein, H. G. Wells, Helen Keller, James Joyce, Leo Tolstoy, and the nineteenth-century German Jewish poet Heinrich Heine, who wrote, 'Where they burn books, they will also ultimately burn people.'

Ava asks her father why the Nazis are burning books. He tells her, '"Because books are dangerous! Nothing opens up the mind and the heart like books do, and so they have the power to change the whole world. That's why they are burning books, Ava. To stop us thinking, and feeling, and imagining . . ." He could not go on. Pulling his handkerchief from his breast pocket, he mopped his eyes and blew his nose. "That is why we must do all we can to resist them, Ava. They would make us robots without a soul." '

When I read, the real world disappears and only the invented world of the book remains. It is like stepping through a gateway into another time or another world, like slipping inside someone else's skin. While I am there, I can dance with dryads, or struggle with my own shadow upon an uncharted sea, or huddle in hiding from a Black Rider. I know what it is like to be a rabbit shivering in the heather, watching my warren being bulldozed. I know how it feels to be poor, obscure, little and plain, yet to love with all my heart. Whatever tribulations I suffer in the world of the book, whatever triumphs I win, they change me as if they had really happened. Whatever I learn returns with me to the real world.

In books, I have lived immeasurable lives. When I was a child, I was such a bookworm that I troubled and bewildered even my very bookish parents. I would borrow six books at a time from the local library, and have read them all by the following day. I used to walk home from school reading. I would become so absorbed in the book that I would walk past my turn-off, and some considerable time later look up, finding myself blocks away from home. I'd miss my stop on train journeys. I would not hear my name being called in class. I would read so late at night that I could hear the kookaburras' weird cackle as I reluctantly turned the last pages.

Much of my childhood is a blur, because I spent so much of it with my nose in a book. Elsewhere. I can, however, remember nearly every book I have ever read, and usually I can remember where I was when I read it. *A Little White Horse* by Elizabeth Goudge was first devoured when I was about ten, in hospital. The walls were bare and discoloured, the linoleum was cracked, and the food was watery and tasteless. How I longed to be at Moonacre Manor, in a bedroom with a vaulted ceiling, delicate ribbings of stone curving over my head like the branches of a tree, sleeping in a four-poster bed hung with pale-blue silk curtains embroidered with silver stars.

How I salivated at the descriptions of supper: 'Home-made crusty bread, hot onion soup, delicious rabbit stew, baked apples in a silver dish, honey, butter the colour of marigolds, a big blue jug of warm mulled claret, and hot roasted chestnuts folded in a napkin.' Over the course of the next few chapters, Maria feasts on sausages, coddled eggs (I did not know what coddled eggs were, but they sounded so delicious), veal-and-ham-and-egg pie, cinnamon syllabub, plum cake, saffron cake, meringues, almond fingers, lemon-curd sandwiches, gingerbread . . . In my imagination I too feasted, and so the paucity and insipidity of the food on my hospital tray was forgotten.

A lot of the books that meant the most to me when I was a child were read in hospital. A childhood accident that destroyed my left tear duct meant I was in and out of the emergency ward constantly. *The Secret Garden* by Frances Hodgson Burnett, *Cue for Treason* by Geoffrey Trease, *The Apple Stone* by Nicholas Stuart Gray and *The Witch's Brat* by Rosemary Sutcliff were all books my mother brought me from our local public library. I devoured them while lying in my narrow metal bed, tucked in tight with hospital corners, a patch over one eye. Always I loved stories of adventure and mystery and magic. My body was kept prisoner by railings and intravenous drips and monitors, but my mind could roam free. It doesn't matter how awful real life is, there is always a way to escape it through the pages of a book.

The summer I read *The Dark is Rising* by Susan Cooper was scorching hot, bare-legs-sticking-to-the-vinyl-car-seat hot. I can still remember the chills that ran all over my body as I read the opening scenes: the sky darkens, the storm gathers and Will hears the whispered words, 'The Walker is abroad . . . this night will be bad and tomorrow will be beyond imagining . . .'

I read *Till We Have Faces: A Myth Untold* by C. S. Lewis in the frangipani tree in the garden of my great-aunts' old fibro cottage, surrounded by the sweet summery smell of the flowers, but inhaling instead the 'temple-smell of blood . . . and burned fat and singed hair and wine and stale incense . . . the Ungit smell.'

The very first teenage party I was ever invited to, I spent the evening hidden behind the curtain in a window-seat reading *Precious Bane* by Mary Webb, a book I had discovered on the host's bookshelf. While everyone else drank and smoked and danced and snogged, and the music thump-thump-thumped, I sat with hare-lipped Prue and listened to 'a still evening with the snow all down, and a green sky, and lambs calling . . . and the crying of the mere when the ice is on it' and the sound of drowned bells coming from under the water.

Leo Tolstoy's *Anna Karenina* was read on a train, after my parents' divorce. The book is full of rocking motion, and dark tunnels, and the shrieking of brakes.

I have read in boats and on beaches and in baths, in trees and on trains and in taxis, in planes and on pony-back and in parks, in cars and bars and spas and bazaars (all true!). I'll read upside down and back-to-front if I have to (the words, not me).

However, reading alone, late at night, is my favourite way. It is such an acute and secret pleasure. All is quiet and dark. Shadows lean over you, but the small light that you read by is a golden globe of protection, a little sun that shines on a multitude of worlds in which anything might happen.

Books are a true kind of magic, and that is why they are so dangerous, and so essential.

'To read a book is to be released into the unbounded sea of mind, as the body to the ocean.'

Giulia Giuffrè

Reading and Secrets

Giulia Giuffrè

Tom [on his way to bed, 1 am]: 'Eh, Giul', you still awaike?'
Giulia: 'I won't be long, Dad, I just want to finish this chapter . . .'

Learning to read

READ ME, A BOOK SAYS TO A CHILD, BUT UNTIL ONE cracks the code, all those black wires are secret and mute. As a reading adult it is only possible to regain that feeling of exclusion by gazing at the patterns of a foreign alphabet. Once the veil lifts on the written word, life is altered forever. The world, already broached by speech, is shattered, thrown up into the air and reformed in a vast rainbow of diamonds; it is articulated – the black ribbon and the black cat are added to the naked body. The cocoon of the child unfurls and suddenly thoughts can be shared across all time and all space.

The learn-to-read books of Giulia's childhood had been laughably remote from a child's quirky world. With titles like *A Book to Read* or *It's Fun to Read*, they introduced the new reader to a stiff world of shadowless categories and bald statements: 'David is a boy.' 'Wendy is a girl.' 'Sue is a little girl.' 'Jump, Nip. See Nip jump.' The tedium of these books would only be relieved on occasion by the unconscious grotesquery of the images.

More recent writers have shown that inventive books for new readers can have an almost compulsive effect: they make the child want to read. And once reading catches, just a sliver or a spark, it grows and grows; the desire feeds the practice feeds the desire. As in learning a foreign language, you know you are succeeding when the impulse to go forward is stronger than any difficulty met along the way. Like a juggernaut, the new reader can plough relentlessly through mispronunciation, difficult names, unknown words. Don't stop. Don't stop. The jigsaw puzzle is three-quarters done and the picture is emerging.

Sophia's note of triumph inside the cover of Enid Blyton's *Mary Mouse on Holiday*, dated 27–6-94: 'I can rrad it.' Texts are no longer monumental, they can change, they can provoke and be interpreted. And the wonder of books that opens out! In perfect plenitude, a mirror of the known world and even more. Everything in the universe has its book image – no subject too obscure, no fantasy too extreme, no idea too opaque but that it has its volume. The key of reading opens up this word-world.

Reading: how and why

What is it to read? Firstly, to read anything at all with any degree of receptivity is a quick and simple therapy for narcissism. Reading offers an escape to another imagination, not simply one's own. By reading, one enters into the experience and vision of other people. This is what lends books their glamour and excitement. Until you read it, you just never really know what a book might contain or where it might lead you. Proust says that reading gives us access to places and times 'one might not have lived through', but, more than this, reading gives us access to people one might not otherwise have been. By ushering a way into multiple lives, reading provides relief from self. To read a book is to be released into the unbounded sea of mind, as the body to the ocean.

Reading can be a refuge from social interaction. *She's home. I think she's reading in the living room.* A person reading is effectively out, not available, *gone readin'*. The act of reading requires attention in order for the spell to take. It can be a defensive activity, shutting out the world as effectively as plunging underwater, blunting observation by others and deflecting emotional arrows. A favourite book is a mental cubbyhouse to which one retreats and within which one relaxes. A safe haven, *b-a-r* spells bar.

With reading comes an independence unknown to the child listening to a story. Suddenly the imaginative portals are unlocked and can be accessed at all times of day or night. Reading is private, personal, secret, isolated, silent. No one can tell if a page has been read or not. Reading is also subversive, because there is no knowing what thought or what image will be unleashed. And it will all happen unseen in one's own head, blessedly unable to be supervised.

Bookshops and libraries are colourful bazaars of the mind. One goes wandering, losing all track of time. The body itself enacts the absorption of the quest – one is not conscious of neck-ache caused by having the head to one side to read titles, of eye-strain and joint-ache, of the distance covered, the stairs climbed, the stretching, the bending and craning. A bookshop is a giant compendium that one travels through, a life-size box of chocolates that draws one further and further in to test and taste. The exploration is only ended by eventual purchase, undeniable exhaustion, insistent hunger or closing time.

Reading is also recognition. In losing ourselves we find ourselves. The books we love – and that is the word we use – are books that speak to us in a congenial way. The authors we seek out or re-read, especially as we get older, are kindred spirits. It is with a kind of wonder that we discover an author who *speaks the same language*. These mind-mates can have been dead for centuries, or live in faraway regions. They can be distant in nearly every way from us and yet here they are now. Moreover in the universe of reading, there is always the heartening possibility of a new voice, a fresh love. Sylvia Townsend Warner's mordant story *Absalom, My Son* portrays a writer, Matthew Bateman, who at the end of his life comes across the book of another writer, Norman Leigh, much younger, now dead. In a description that incidentally suggests Townsend Warner's own mind, Bateman is struck by the similarity of Leigh's book to his own work:

> *Reverse the Sun* seriously delighted him . . . At times he stopped quite uncritically, halted by sheer astonishment at finding something so unforeseeably well managed. Yet though the book astonished him, it was congenial too, the fruit of a congenial mind: a scrupulous, searching, disdainful mind, with a vein of black bile.

The affinity is so great that Bateman cannot decide if it is kinship or plagiarism. In any case he concludes with a sense of bereavement that 'Norman Leigh, writing like Matthew Bateman, had written a better book than ever Matthew Bateman had set his name to', and the rest of the story lightly, grittily traces the consequences of this realisation.

Through their books writer-friends can provide a powerful salve for loneliness, second in efficacy only to writing itself. Where else can you choose your companions completely at will, suiting choice to mood with unmitigated sway? Proust describes the free, private dialogue one can have with writers as the best of company in the heart of solitude: '*ce miracle fécond d'une communication au sein de la solitude . . .*' Everyone who likes to read has an inner circle of favourite authors, a close and special band of books often ranged beside the bed in a gesture of intimacy. The desert island books game is a test for this: what are the last six books you would retain in a wilderness? What is the final book you would surrender?

There is another way in which reading assuages loneliness and it is in the recognition one can have of one's own fears and joys in what one reads. A chord is struck, a resonance intoned. Reading gives you other things to recall that you have lived in your head. This enriches the life memory-brew many times over. Reading souvenirs can be a whole book, a phrase, a poem, an image, a feeling-from-words with as distinct and evocative a taste as a first oyster. From early reading one gleans scraps of mental furniture for every mood and eventuality: always a mantra of comfort the words 'Do not let your heart be troubled'; for laughter, G. K. Chesterton's unfailingly funny conclusion to an analysis of vegetarianism and veganism, 'Why should Salt suffer?'; for rhapsodic wonder at the world, Gerard Manley Hopkins; for uninhibited humorous intelligence, Proust; for self-dramatisation, Sterne; and so on, *ad infinitum*.

A secondary pleasure of reading is talking about the book, especially with someone who admires it, but also when there is thoughtful disagreement. Reading shared by discussion afterwards increases the companionship of books. There is an absolute appeal in working out through a dialectic of discussion, argument, joke, interruption, confluence, recantation *exactly* what one thinks about a particular book and why. Open discussion of books and ideas with others – by far the best part of a university arts degree – can enhance the solitary pleasure of reading.

As when you sleep, the sensation of time passing stops when you are reading. The absorption can be absolute. Reading is like a meditation. Hours pass, mealtimes come and go, the morning light changes to that of the afternoon and then the evening, the night changes to dawn. But one is only subliminally aware of these things – the mind and heart are in the book. This is the experience that people are seeking when they wander through a bookshop or a library: what will grab them, and take them out of their own time into that blissful reading state.

It is a paradox of reading that we seek beautiful, comfortable places to read – a hammock in a shady summer garden, a big armchair beside a fire in winter – so that we can then forget where we are. But the memory is not so much obliterated as encoded and filed away, often with the book itself. Proust says that this 'lost time' of childhood, of being completely absorbed in a book ostensibly oblivious to everything else, actually makes us remember the times and places of the reading. The film of a child reading would be like time-lapse photography of someone sleeping: many different positions are taken that at the time the sleeper (or reader) is not aware of, but later, memory of the reading can bring back the physical sensations. The weight and awkwardness of big, fat paperbacks read sideways in bed; the ease of reading plastic-covered hardback novels from the library while draped this way and that on a sofa; even sometimes reading upside down with one's legs over the back of the sofa and the book held up in front of the face; the difficulty of reading in the fierce Australian sun – the technique of using your own head-shadow as a light by which to read the book; reading on a boat with the wave-motion in your body, the hum of the engine in your ears and a smell of mildewed plastic in your nostrils; reading in a tree with air around your head; on the beach hearing the scratchy sound of sand granules whipping the page; reading while eating; reading on the toilet; reading in the bath, always more desirable an idea than enjoyable a practice. Giulia remembered reading in Linacre Library in Oxford – when it was still on St Aldate's – one cold winter's day in 1976. The night before, it had snowed, but now it was clear and frosty. That particular day – warmth, books and papers inside, a lofty white diffused light and crunchy snow covering everything outside – imprinted itself on her as an emblem of the utter joy of reading books.

The bookmark becomes a companion to reading travels, a modest constancy. Until she was eight or so Giulia marked the place by turning down the corner of the page. But one afternoon, as she was sitting on her school-case reading and waiting for her mother to pick her up from school, Mother Declan, a short, powerful, husky-voiced, red-faced Irish nun, the head of the Infant division of the convent, came upon her and said, 'What are you reading, dear? Oh, goodness, you wouldn't be marking the place by bending the page, would you, dear? That shows you have no respect for the book.' From that day on, Giulia never, ever bent the corner of a book page, and she reprimanded Sophia for doing the same thing:

> 'Sophia, don't, you'll make dog-ears.'
> 'But Mum, there's only one.'

Not all reading is completely absorbed. With age comes flicking, and speed-reading, and quick-review reading – all styles of reading that enable your attention to come and go and provide an overview. There was even a joke in the English Department at Sydney University when Giulia was teaching there: 'Read it? I haven't even lectured on it!'

You do not have to finish a book. That is one of the beauties of reading. When a lecture starts, or a movie or a sermon, a kind of narrative claustrophobia can set in. With a book you can escape by simply closing the volume and putting it down. Or you can skim through the rest, or stop with a bookmark exclamation frozen forever a quarter of an inch into the volume. Interest is the main requirement of any book, for that is what keeps you reading at all; and in fact if you are forced by sheer skill and energy to read all the words on the page, as opposed to skating along, then you find you are *listening*.

Addiction to reading

> Sophia (16) to Giulia: 'If reading made you lose weight, you'd be thin as!'

In some people the love of reading becomes a complete obsession. The short-sighted can always relax from seeing by taking off their glasses or removing their contact lenses, thereby blurring the world into surround. Those addicted to reading, however, find it almost impossible to stop. They might well put down an individual book, but to stop reading altogether – impossible. You might almost say they have a fear of not reading. For these people, to live is to read.

And they will read everything. Like the gentleman with a weakness for wood, they will devour all printed matter around them before they search further afield. Giulia was and remained one such addict. Into her Kensington household came regularly the following material for her to read cover to cover: the *Sydney Morning Herald*, the *Sun-Herald*, the *Catholic Weekly*, the *National Times*, *Australian Women's Weekly*, *Reader's Digest*, the *Smoke Signal* (the Marrickville Rotary journal with cover designed by Tom). Cereal packets, record covers, recipe books – all grist to the mill. When away from the house Giulia always carried two books. What if you finished the one you were reading? She kept large scrapbooks of clippings, and covered the walls of her tiny study with articles and pictures culled from the papers. Anything odd, interesting, affecting. To this day, the same obsession:

> Orlando (12) to Giulia, reading and cutting out clippings on the dining room table: 'What are you doing, Mum? Is this what your life has come to? Are you seeking vainly for some reference to yourself? Other people read a newspaper and then throw it out. You take it to pieces and keep it. What use is that? You come across some old article. You read – ah, they opened the bridge! So what? It's been, it's gone. It's later, too late!'

Unrepentant, incorrigible in this unswitch-off-able propensity to interpret, Giulia continued to read on.

For someone with Giulia's Gemini personality, reading was a balm. It provided a quiet other place to be when vivacity palled, or a profound relief from the crying jags of her adolescence. Left entirely to herself Giulia would easily turn in on herself and consume herself with anxiety: a book, a pen, a notebook stopped that at once and gave instant access to the rest of the world. The aim, to be absorbed in a book, everyday reality running on as an accompaniment. The joyfulness of the realisation that there are so many books, that if you were to read every minute of every day that remained to you, you could not run out. That you do not have to read books in any order – though some dogged people do attempt to work through the alphabet in a library; that the worldwide web of books is unruly and non-hierarchical. That at any time you might *discover* a new fresh, beautiful writer to add to your collection. The rapture of finding a congenial author who, better still, has written a series of books. You know then that your trail for the next while is mapped out. The emptiness of finishing a book – the volume changing abruptly from its generous open form back into a self-contained box. The strange mourning that accompanies the last pages of the book. From hastening through the book to a kind of slow-motion languor at the end, knowing full well that to finish the book will mean the end of that emotional journey. While deep in a particular book, the rest of life is coloured by that author's mind, and whatever one is doing, the book is on standby, one's place marked, waiting for the next immersion. That book throws other things into definition as 'non-book, various'.

Often Giulia would read late into the night. Sometimes she would read under the bedcovers with a torch so that the tell-tale rectangle of light around the bedroom door would not disclose that she was still up reading. The danger time was always around 1 or 2 am when Tom came to bed, past her room, past the jingling grandfather clock in the hall to the parental bedroom next door. If one could lie low for that, it was then safe to read until dawn. Just one more chapter, and another. How could one stop when it was so interesting? How could one have the perfidy to leave that newfound friend, the author, to abandon that other created world?

On the bookshelves at Kensington – tellingly kept in the added-on, uncosy *wintergarden* – was a very odd set of books, significant only in that somehow they had all arrived there, and once there, remained seemingly forever – never added to in the dynamism of a living library. From Dr Rumble's *Radio Replies*, *The Encyclopaedia Britannica*, a Shakespeare and Kobbé's *Complete Opera Book* to *Peoples of the World in Pictures*, a slab of *Reader's Digests*, Lin Yutang's *The Importance of Living*, Benvenuto Cellini's *Autobiography*, Edward Bulwer-Lytton's

The Last Days of Pompeii and Osbert Sitwell's *Laughter in the Next Room*. There were some technical design books like *The Australian Flora in Applied Art, Part 1, The Waratah* by R. T. Baker, Marie's old Italian grammar, and French and Latin dictionaries; and there were a few books from Nonno Vincenzo's vast library, including *Camille* (read in 1919, *Degno di una seconda lettura, V. Giuffrè, Australia, 1925.* Worth a second reading), Tasso's *Opere* and his English editions of Pope and Milton. On the top shelf, solemn sentinel to this static collection, sixteen volumes of the handsome black, silver and gold Richard Burton's *Arabian Nights, The Book of the Thousand Nights and a Night, Alflaylah Wa Laylah.*

When Giulia was growing up, there was not a lot of reading going on in the immediate family. Nonna would occasionally read a newspaper or a magazine with absolute frowning concentration, using her magnifying glass, and licking her finger to turn the page. Tom would read the newspapers, a business report, or an engineering manual, but lightly, osmotically. What he loved were television programs about the ocean or fish, even *Seahunt* would do. He only had to hear the first unmistakeable chorus of underwater bubbles on the soundtrack to come running to the TV set from the most remote corner of the house. 'Why don't you just buy a fish, Dad?' Giulia had once joked. Bruno loved the *How and Why Book* series, and science fiction. Marie, and then in her turn Sonia, took the road paved with the thick pink bricks of the romance novel. Every night Marie would take a small glass of Fernet Branca, as bitter as her book was sweet, and curl up with her current Mills & Boon . . . *I just want to unwind.*

Childhood books

What is it that makes some books imbibed early in life so potent that their flavours remain to act as unconscious standards for us, like personalised versions of the weights and measures kept at Greenwich? The books of childhood do remind us of ourselves when young. They remind us of the days when the summers used to be so long, of days of real leisure – only faintly reproduced in times of adult holiday now – days when one could read and read without stopping for any duty, or for anyone.

But, more than this, some books of childhood actually had – and continue to have – a completely delicious taste. They really are like a magical food. All passionate readers have their own list of childhood favourites. Giulia's would include the 'Susan' books, *Anne of Green Gables*, *The Swiss Family Robinson*, Mary Grant Bruce's *Billabong* books, *The Secret Seven* and *The Famous Five* books, Louisa May Alcott's *Little Women*, and more especially her *An Old-Fashioned Girl*; *The Wind in the Willows*, Katy, Alice, Pollyanna, Cherry Ames, the Bobbsey twins; an *honorary* book of her childhood, read as an adult but which undoubtedly would have been one of the loved ones, Tove Jansson's *The Summer Book*; P. G. Wodehouse's stories; girls' school stories without end; half-forgotten but still haunting books about an Aboriginal detective, or a clever, intrepid boy detective with an older sister, or a book set in the clarity of the Arizona desert.

One of Giulia's favourite books, Enid Blyton's *The Magic Faraway Tree*, was itself a metaphor for the reading process: marvellous, totally different lands arriving at the top of the tree – the Land of Spells, the Land of Do As You Please, the Land of Goodies – that intrigue the children completely for a time, but that would then disappear in the winds of darkness and change, to be replaced by another magic place. The young protagonists of the tale, Dick, Fanny and Jo [Orlando and Sophia: 'Dick and Fanny!'] are joined in their adventures by a mixed group of fantastical creatures, and it is part of Blyton's brilliance to normalise the magical, so it becomes all the more seductive. The pleasure of *The Magic Faraway Tree* also derives in no small part from the inherent danger for the children: if they were to miss the timing of their exit at the top of the tree – or, like greedy Dick, became too big to fit through the escape-hatch (surely a fear-fantasy of the inability to be born) – the visiting land would whirl on nonetheless, and then where would they be? Nowhere, lost forever in an interval . . .

Enid Blyton has the gift of giving her characters the autonomy that her child readers most desire, or at least most desired and did not have in the 1950s and '60s. The Secret Seven and the Famous Five have meetings and make their own decisions, weigh up risks and take them, piece together clues and solve riddling crimes that have the police baffled. They direct their own lives. *Five Go Off in a Caravan* opens with the children deciding where to go for their summer holidays, at an age when Giulia was hardly allowed to walk down to the Kensington shops for a bottle of milk! Parents are excitingly irrelevant. The bonds between the children are far more important. Even Timmy the dog, who is the fifth of the Five, is more reliable and 'trustable' (to use Blyton's term) than the remote adults. Mothers really only exist in the world of the books to provide 'delumptious and scruplicious' provisions. Or they are sick, in another country, or dead. Fathers hardly figure, and when they do they are grumpy, abstracted and involved in high-powered secret, cerebral work of their own. In short, the adults are absent from the ambit of their children to a degree which is nothing short of miraculous to anyone with even the slightest acquaintance with *la famiglia italiana*.

These childhood adventure books revolve around mystery. Key words are quest, discovery, secret, stolen, locked, sinister, study, drawer, treasure, imposter, clue, surprise, forbidden, mystery. *The Secret Garden*, *The Secret of Greycliffs*, *The Mystery of the Silver Circle*, *The Secret Study*, *The Secret Seven*. There is the secret that the child or children investigate. There is the even more important matter of keeping a secret from the parents in the book, and eventually there is the secret of the readers of the books from their own real parents, hitherto uncharted territory.

At the same time, coexisting no matter how precariously with that impulse to independence, parental approval is still vital. Far from getting into trouble for their adventurousness, these children are beamed upon and congratulated, truly the stuff of marvellous child fantasy: 'The Inspector left at last, beaming, full of admiration once more for the Secret Seven . . . "Smart bit of work you children did," said the Inspector approvingly.' The very book titles are pats on the back:

> *Good Work Secret Seven*
> *Three Cheers Secret Seven*
> *Leslie Wins Through*
> *Doris Finds the Way*
> *Monica Turns up Trumps*

A few specifically Australian books came one's way in these days of childhood reading. Some might as well have been English. In *The Family at Willow Bend* by Helen Fowler, for instance, the scene is very much the English one, the mentality obstinately so. Lance rejects a Ned Kelly dress-up costume: '"cover my attractive aquiline features with one of those tin-can things!" he said indignantly, "and besides, he was a criminal."' He opts for Robin Hood instead. And Christmas festivities must make no concession to the heat of an Australian summer – Monica finds her sister in the laundry making angel outfits for the Christmas play:

> 'Kit, it's too hot,' she said compassionately when she saw Kit's delicate, scarlet-flushed face above a mound of billowing starched white voile.
>
> 'It's got to be done, Monica,' Kit replied. 'The angels must look spick-and-span, heatwave or no heatwave.'

Mary Grant Bruce's *Billabong* series of books carried with them a welcome scent of eucalyptus and the colours and light of rural Australia. We are out of the drawing room and into the paddocks, the wind in our collective hair. There is the sound of full laughter, not just smiling, or twinkling or being jolly pleased. Norah, Jim and Wally are strong, healthy, young, spirited and Australian. Their images are as attractive and idealised as the iconic murals that used to adorn

Australian pubs. Oh, to have a funny, protective, teasing, boyish yet manly older brother like Jim, a potential friend/lover as appealing, playful and brave as Wally, or to be as independent, capable, womanly, courageous and feeling as Norah! In these books the descriptions and the attitude went some way towards interpreting a country back to itself, so that it could be seen not simply in a colonial mirror image.

A little authenticity went a long way at this time, helping one to store up a set of lenses for the future. Kenneth Slessor celebrated urban Australia, and created a vision of the lovable tawdry glamour of Sydney streets, especially in the rain and the dark. His moody evocation of Sydney Harbour in 'Five Bells' continues to resonate. Patricia Wrightson was another writer who tapped into Australianness at this time. *The Rocks of Honey* even broaches Australia's ancient aspect, and offers an early treatment of reconciliation themes. Another specifically Australian childhood book, a great favourite of Giulia's, was Marian Warren's *No Glamour in Gumboots.* This comic *tour de force* is the story of one woman's unsuccessful attempt at duck farming in the south-west of Sydney. The book is irreverent, realistic and life-affirming. It is also an early and good attempt at conveying the multicultural society on the (then) fringes of Sydney. The heroine has Warren's fascination (not always benign) with people and this lends her descriptions a trenchant accuracy, but alongside this satiric impulse is a facility with words that can only be described as loving.

But by and large, how English were most of these school-story books, and school magazines like *The Girls' Crystal* and the eagerly awaited *Girls' Crystal Annual.* The illustrations were girls' own to the last cross-hatching. The language was totally and distinctively not Australian. Endorsement, for example, would be regularly expressed by saying things like, 'How perfectly, perfectly lovely! How absolutely topping! You are a brick. You do have lots of spunk!' and 'Mmmm, how scrummy! Gorgeous chocs, thank you, Mother.'

Violence in these books about school life is suppressed to an almost hilarious degree, and yet once the reader tunes into the register, the smallest gesture could seem cataclysmic. Dispossessed by her wicked cousin, an out-of-control Alison 'gave the embroidery frame a rebellious push'. In *Alison Temple – Prefect* Jane is immeasurably shocked to see the social structure undone by the destruction of a half-completed tricky jigsaw puzzle.

What happens when an Italo-Australian girl reads a lot of books that are almost preternaturally English – books wherein the very first sentence of Chapter One might begin: 'Alison and Jane had been primrosing in the spinney . . .' (What's primrosing? What's a spinney?) One could be surrounded by Australia in all its particularity – light, sun, the dear colours; one could have Italian blood, body and customs; at the same time one could be drenched in the Irish Catholicism of the Brigidine nuns; and yet in one's private mental space there were green English fields, hockey matches and hearty, tender girl companions a world away. And the descriptions could cause a profound nostalgia for a pretty landscape and a cultural safety one had never actually experienced. These British school stories provided a childhood mental home so very far removed from your actual life. It was like enacting in your own being the colonial saga of the entire nation. The only thing to be said for this profound cultural dislocation was that, if you could survive it, it did give you the ability to live in several worlds at the same time.

Louisa May Alcott's *An Old-Fashioned Girl* was one of the few books Giulia used to re-read. As an adult looking through its saccharine pages, she found it difficult to recapture its magic. The good-natured music teacher from the country, Polly, is just so kind and needed by everyone else. Her creative thrift in turning gowns and recycling bonnets is attractive and daunting at the same time, her steel-bright authenticity challenging. But there is one scene in the book that stands out even now: a droll, impromptu studio picnic of women artists. Polly takes the superficial and manipulative Fanny along, and we see a lot of the scene through her sceptical and then admiring eyes. The scene stands out for its unsentimental feminism.

The women make their own society and their own art. They are real, strong, they are artists, and they are good-humoured with it. There are no male reference points whatsoever.

The impression of this blithe women's working lunch remained with Giulia: the depiction of the woman artist as a particular kind of hero, one who could be somewhat bohemian – invent her own life, not live according to a pre-ordained template – and remain an observing but far from detached outsider.

Sophia (13) to Giulia, on reading the title of this chapter, 'Reading and Secrets': 'Ooooh, what secrets? Tell me . . . what are the secrets?'

Sophia again, eyes widening, when looking at some of Giulia's notes headed 'secrets – generic': 'Ooooh, old secrets, passed down from generation to generation. They're the best, they're the most juicy . . .'

'I read so I didn't have to think about where I was, or why I was there, or what I would do next. I read to be seduced.'

Carrie Tiffany

Wessex

Carrie Tiffany

I LEARNT TO READ IN THE DESERT. I WAS TWENTY years old and working as a park ranger in central Australia. I lived in a silver caravan stumped up with old house bricks. During the day I emptied the rubbish bins, or went on patrol, or took tourists on guided walks, or shot feral cats. At night I read books.

Books were scarce in the desert. The national park I worked on was serviced by a tourist resort that sold flyspray and wafer-thin boomerangs made in China. It did not sell books. The nearest books were in a library 400 kilometres away. I rang the library and joined up as a remote reader. Books would be sent out to me every month on one of the tourist buses. I couldn't access the catalogue so a librarian would choose the books on my behalf. My librarian was called Merv. I wrote him a note with a summary of my tastes. But I was twenty – it was the summary of a taste I had not yet acquired.

The books arrived one afternoon on a Greyhound bus with a dozen Swedes, some Germans and Japanese. I was still in my ranger uniform and it went badly. The tourists thought I had come to meet them, not to collect a box of books, so I had to explain. They nodded and smiled. They wanted to see the books. I held each one in front of me for a few seconds while they squinted at the covers and mouthed the titles. They looked disappointed. It was the wrong detail in the holiday stories tourists tell about rangers. I should have been collecting medical supplies, or an important part to repair the two-way radio. I took the books back to my caravan and turned on the air conditioner. *Turtles of the Top End*, *Practical First Aid*, *Leyland Brothers Trekabout* and Thea Astley's *The Well Dressed Explorer.*

I read so as not to feel alone, and to escape the heat. There were months of forty-degree days. The air felt too hot to ingest – like it was pulsing off metal. I sniffed and panted. The blood vessels in my nostrils hardened and sprung leaks. My pockets were full of rusty tissues. When I washed the blood stains from my shirts and hung them on the line, they snap-dried in seconds.

I rationed *The Well Dressed Explorer.* Fifteen pages in bed at night, three with breakfast. When I came back to my caravan after a day's work I felt a surge of relief that *The Explorer* was still there, high and dry on its scatter of toast crumbs. I sent Merv a note asking for more stories like Astley's. The next Greyhound bus brought Eleanor Dark, Christina Stead and Patrick White.

I didn't read in front of the other rangers, and I certainly didn't talk about reading. We talked about the day we were in, and the days immediately before and after. The roster was ten days on, four days off, so we talked about where we were in the roster and if we would go to town on our days off. As I came to the end of a ten-day roster I would use a pocket calculator to see if I had enough pages to cover my days off. I could not imagine a day when I did not read.

There were real stories in the desert. Stories as engaging as anything I was reading, but somehow their very realness prevented me from entering them.

An Anangu woman I worked with told me the story of her life in a liquid mixture of English and Pitjantjatjara. The woman wasn't exactly from the country of this national park, but some other country a few hours' drive away. She had come here as a teenager and was taken in by a white man working as a mechanic at one of the roadhouses. She kept the man's house and had a daughter with him. The mechanic was a short-termer – a man from down south who'd come to the Territory to make money and escape for a while. When he left he took the child, but not her mother. The Anangu woman didn't know where they had gone, or how she might find them. She had never been more than a few hours from the mission she was born on. She couldn't read, or dial the numbers on a telephone. She went to the courthouse (next to the library) in the town that was 400 kilometres away to ask the judge to return her child, but crippled with fear and shyness she was unable to speak.

The Anangu woman moved back into the Aboriginal community and eventually married again. She lived on the fringe of the two worlds – working with the whites as a ranger during the day and living in the community at night. By the time she was twelve the daughter had moved back to central Australia. She was living in a hostel and going to high school in the 400-kilometre-away town from where her mother worked on the national park. They saw each other occasionally but the daughter spoke only English – the language her mother had needed to save her, but didn't have.

One day I gave the mother a lift to town. She asked me to stop at the high school. I waited behind the wheel as she walked up and down behind the fence watching the children playing on the red dirt oval. I saw her motion with her hands and a tall girl wearing purple sneakers kicked her way across to us. The mother put the girl in the back seat and told me to drive out of town to the east. We drove for several hours along the bitumen then we left the road and picked our way slowly along a dry creek bed. We passed through a stand of desert oaks. The mother began to hit the heel of her hand rhythmically against the dashboard. She started to sing in her language. The mother was singing the country to her daughter – reading the story of the landscape to her. I looked in the rear-view mirror. The daughter sat slumped over her Walkman tracing the little plastic sprocket at its centre with her nail-polished finger. She was wearing her headphones; she was deaf to the story.

I read so I didn't have to see what was in front of me. This was nothing new. As a teenager I used reading as a weapon against my mother. I chose books on the basis that she couldn't pronounce the name of the author. The Russians got a good go – Dostoyevsky, Turgenev, Solzhenitsyn. And I liked thickness. Great dense loaves of books that made my mother's Georgette Heyers and Mills & Boons look like white bread slices. We were a television house, not a book house. The great writers of my family's heyday were TV comics like Dave Allen and the Two Ronnies. My father's only books were car servicing manuals and a couple of leather-bound Dickens he had bought in a junk shop just before we left England. My father figured he'd make a serious profit by selling the second-hand Dickens in Australia. Three months later, when our shipping container arrived, my father was already an Australian. I unwrapped the books from our winter sheets and placed them on a shelf in my bedroom where they gave off an unmistakable smell of England – of gravy.

I read to protect myself against the dark. During the day I told the tourists about the rich nocturnal life of the desert. I described pythons chaining across the cooling sands, bilbies emerging from their burrows to feed in the starlight, owls coasting on thermals between the dunes. But the nights inside my caravan were tame. The stale air rotated backwards and forwards through the air conditioner. The only sound was the turning of pages, the rearranging of limbs and pillows, and an occasional break for tea. I did not like the gap of time between reading and sleep. When I closed the book and turned off the light I was returned to myself, jarred and suspended.

I read of one landscape and lived in another. On my twenty-first birthday Merv sent me a card to say he was taking me to England.

George Eliot, Jane Austen, Thomas Hardy, the Brontës. My country. I read of moors, fens, dells and heaths.

Sometimes there were strange echoes between what I read and what I was doing. I read Thomas Hardy's *The Return of the Native* in a bird hide with blood on my hands. We were researching the wedge-tailed eagles that flew up and down the highways feeding on roadkill, and in the process often becoming roadkill themselves. A lump of horsemeat was staked out near a road and the rangers took turns recording observations in a tiny hide dug into the ground and covered with sticks and spinifex. Each ranger took a four-hour shift writing down how many eagles arrived and how long they fed for. When the horsemeat ran out, a new fetid and maggoty lump had to be dragged out from under a tarpaulin some distance away.

The eagles were fast and vicious. Their feathers stuck together in greasy clumps. They had sharp beaks and huge drumstick legs. Once a group had gathered they fed and fought each other. I wrote my observations every twenty minutes or so, but the rest of the time I made a pillow from the red sand and rolled onto my back to read. I read about Diggory Venn, Thomas Hardy's reddleman in *The Return of the Native*, a peddler who digs up red clay to make dye for sheep's wool. The clay seeps into his skin leaving a permanent red stain. Venn is a native of Edgon Heath – a desolate flatland in Hardy's Wessex. When I rolled over to check the eagles through the viewing slit in the bird hide my eyes took a few seconds to readjust, to push back the image of Diggory Venn the reddleman. I returned *The Return of the Native* to Merv at the library with blood smears on many of the pages from where I had touched the horsemeat. I didn't feel especially guilty and it was beyond me to explain.

I read so I didn't have to think about where I was, or why I was there, or what I would do next. I read to be seduced. Merv went on a librarians' study tour of Paris. He sent me Hugo, Dumas and Flaubert's *Madame Bovary*. I fell badly for Flaubert. I read *Madame Bovary* three times. It was hard to put it back on the bus. I noticed the nametag of the girl serving behind the counter at the roadhouse: Emma. She wore blue eye shadow and Australian flag earrings, but I still looked at her anew. The French books had advertisements in the back for other titles. I liked the sound of *Remembrance of Things Past* by Marcel Proust. I wrote a request to Merv and he obliged. I was late for the bus and my books had been left on the side of the road. Not the one book by the writer Proust that I had expected, but seven – a great bale of books tilting in the afternoon sun.

Sometimes a story from the day attached itself to the book I was reading at night, and I felt the book and the story were in conversation through me. I was reading *Capricornia* by Xavier Herbert and working to build a walking track with my friend, the Anangu woman. My friend talked about her daughter. She had left high school and gone back down south. She wondered if her daughter had a boyfriend now, or a baby. *Capricornia* ends when the body of a pregnant Aboriginal girl is discovered in an empty water tank. The girl had hidden in the tank out of fear her child would be taken away. As my friend talked of her daughter I could see the dessicated body of the girl in the tank – the desperate marks her fingernails had made as she scratched at the rusty corrugated iron. It was too hot to be building a walking track. My friend's story, with the images from the book attached, was too much for me. I said I wasn't feeling well. I said we should knock off early.

Reading in the desert is not the same as reading in the classroom or at a university. My knowledge of the world, of history and politics and geography, was poor. Everything to me was at the same time both fictional and real.

After a few years I left my job as a park ranger in the desert and went back to England to visit my relatives. I was in London during December and had a few days to kill before Christmas. I was reading the Latins then – humid books by García Márquez and Allende and Paz, but I was thinking about Thomas Hardy. I went to the ticket office at the tube station and asked how I would get to Wessex. One

British Rail employee consulted another and then another. A young Indian woman finally broke it to me gently. The Wessex made famous by the English writer Thomas Hardy was not a real place. It was a place only in books. It existed in the imagination. It was not possible to go there.

'By digesting books, I am creating myself.
You are what you read.'

MALCOLM KNOX

This Is Your Life

Malcolm Knox

WE WERE COMING IN TO LAND, BUT THE MAN ACROSS the aisle continued to read his ebook. My ears popping, my palms sweating, I considered a word.

'Excuse me. I'm sure you have investigated the actual effects of electronic devices being in use while an aircraft is descending, and I'm sure you have satisfied yourself that they have as much influence on navigation systems as picking your nose . . . But *please*, you are asking me and four hundred strangers to trust you on this. Is it fair to expect us to take the odds?'

I remained silent. By the time I had stammered my mealy-mouthed plea, half incoherent with shyness, half fuming with anger, the plane would have landed. Or crashed. It was too late.

And now it is too late. You no longer have to turn off your electronic device when a plane is taking off or landing. It's another blow to the printed book or, as it's called, the p-book. Old people like me are already looking back nostalgically to those minutes, about twenty of them on either side of lift-off and touch-down, when the paper book *killed* the ebook, the iPad, the smartphone and every other device, those minutes when the paper book ruled the air.

But there is something more than that, something very important that has been lost.

Back to the man on the plane. What bugged me, even more than his blithely taking a life-and-death risk on all of our behalf, was that I couldn't tell what he was reading. Without the clue of a cover (embossed or sober?) or a format (brick-sized airport paperback, slim novella or scholarly tome?), I had no idea how to talk to him. An essential clue to our common humanity had been lost. Would I have talked to him differently knowing he was reading Matt Reilly, as opposed to Richard Flanagan? Stephenie Meyer, as opposed to Alexis Wright? Sadly, yes, and sadder still, without a book cover through which to read the man, I was silenced. All I knew for sure was that he was so gripped by this book, it was worth risking lives for. If he was that much of a reader, maybe he was a man I could have spoken with.

For many years, I fought the ebook tide. I knew I should do it – for the trees, for the carbon footprint, for the thrill of novelty to which I am no more immune than the next person. I have Kindle on my iPad, and when travelling will load it up with books. It gives me a glutton's buzz to have a library in my hands; if I ever grow bored with one book I can switch to another without thinking of cost or weight. I am happy to read on a screen. The device saves me from one of my deepest fears: that I will be caught somewhere, stuck with nothing to do, without a book to read, a fear that affects me as profoundly as a Depression-raised child used to worry about going hungry. I sock away emergency books the way my grandmother used to store tinned food. You never knew when you'd need it. The ebook answers our prayers, but still . . . still . . . I can't quite do it. When I come home from a trip, if I am reading a book on the device, I will go out and buy a print version and continue from there. I will even buy the print versions of the ebooks I have finished while away. When I am not travelling, I do not read a single book electronically.

I wonder if, when I was a child and first enchanted by books, digital files would have cast the same spell. My son, now twelve, reads books on his iPad, but it's clear that he sees these as the bitter medicinal doses he has to take between the serious business of playing games. Their being on the same device makes books marginally more palatable, but only marginally. I was more like my daughter, who at eleven wolfs down books – print books, with pictures, a couple of years below her reading level – as if filling an emptiness. I was that kind of reader, indiscriminate, hedonistic and insatiable, reading first and asking questions later, harvesting swathes of trash and comics and illustrated books and fun stuff for years and years before I ever sat down with a 'serious' book, whatever that was. Like my daughter, I was a great big garbage-guts.

The further from 'Recommended Reading', the better. My guides through my tweens were Frederick Forsyth, Mario Puzo, James Michener, Leon Uris and James Clavell, not to mention a long overhang of cartoons and picture books. I remember the loss of innocence of reading John Irving's *The World According to Garp*: scarcely had I got over the shock that a woman could put her adulterous lover's penis in her mouth in his car, when there was an accident, a shunt, and she bit it off. That was more than a kid should have to take in. Who knows what scars it left? Either way, I was not only a lover of trash, but I loved showing it off. At eleven, to carry around my copy of *The Godfather*, face-out to the crowd, was as big a show of maturity as I could think of.

Those growing-up years are pretty interesting, because when you believe one thing, a month later you'll be absolutely convinced of its opposite. I liked people seeing what I was reading, and the next moment I was terrified of being caught.

Racy novels filled the shelves of the two big readers in our family, my father and my maternal grandmother, Lilian Walker. It shocks me more now than it did then, the amount of Irving Wallace, Jackie Collins and Harold Robbins they went through – cripes, the inner lives of 1970s adults! Had they been reading ebooks, surely such material would have been hidden behind some kind of parental lock. Wallace's tied-up supermodel sex slaves and Robbins' depraved billionaires were a new avenue of access to the adult world, just as exciting as Uris's Holocaust or Michener's Hawaii, but taboo. And you could see them on the outside! The more I felt I had to hide what I was reading, the more books felt like the centre of the universe. What was important was their *substance*, right down to the fat saucy title and the picture on the cover.

The materiality of books, I suspect, goes some way to explain why I get into a real state if I am, or fear I might be, caught somewhere without one. I need the book in my bag or in my hands as much as a toddler needs his blankie and goes on needing it right through childhood. I have an uncle, my father's brother Hugh, who is so wedded to his book of the moment that when visitors go to his flat to see him, he will spend a couple of minutes greeting and seating them, before he settles into an armchair and continues his reading. If he goes out with friends on the train, he does not talk, but reads his book. Uncle Hugh is in his eighties. If I live that long, he is my future.

This is going to sound a bit dumb and boyishly materialistic, but I came to see the physical solidity of books as desirable, and ultimately signifying a worthwhile life, as someone else might see cars, or property, or money itself. I don't know how, when or why this started. I do recall that when my paternal grandmother, Bessie Alice Knox, died, one of the biggest bones of contention between my father and his three siblings was her book collection. It included Cole's *Funny Picture Book* that my brother and I used to go and look at, and very old folk children's books such as the delectably horrifying *Der Struwwelpeter*, but it also had a lot of encyclopedia sets, two metres of leather-bound Dickens, and many other items of undeniable importance. I don't know what kind of estate she left, but the only thing her children fought about was who got her books.

My great-aunt, Dorothy Knox, was the other grande dame of that side of the family. Though blind, she was an eminent woman and our matriarch, and when we visited her she was ensconced in her flat surrounded by floor-to-ceiling shelves of hardback books. I never read any of them, and obviously she didn't need them anymore, but the *mise en scène* left a deep imprint. She could see nothing, but she was not going to let go of a single book. I never forgot that setting, the majesty of Aunt Dorothy enthroned among books. When I was twelve, I had to go for a consultation with a heart surgeon, and there and then I decided what I wanted to be when I grew up. I don't think it was surgery that attracted me – in fact, I know it wasn't. What I liked was the idea of being ensconced in a room, behind a desk, the four walls around me filled by heavy books. They were lined up perfectly like a communist army, and he was its general.

Books inflamed me; they were seductive, whether in the family-love way of my great-aunt, the masculine course-charting way of the surgeon, or literally seductive, as when I see a woman in public reading, say, something as heart-breaking as *Pale Fire* or as funny as *A Confederacy of Dunces* or as consuming as *Anna Karenina*. Nothing sexier! The electronic book robs us of that chance to fall in love, or at least to feel less alone in the universe.

As devoted as I became to the materiality of books, I grew proportionately scornful of those who would fake the look. Eliot and Dickens would join me in mocking the gentleman whose library was stocked with their untouched volumes. I remember, as an adult, sneering at real estate inspections of dignified houses with bookshelves blatantly furnished with unread filler, as shallow as false spines. I once had a flatmate who, before entertaining girlfriends in his bedroom, artfully arranged Penguin Classics face-up on the floor around his bed as design items. Here I wasn't sneering so much as jealous – he was stealing *my* thing, for *his* advantage! If those girls were really impressed by Plato's *Last Days of Socrates*, surely they would be engaged in dialogue with me, not that charlatan in the next room!

While I cared – perhaps too much – for books, I didn't look after them well. Mine are the books with rain-swollen pages, coffee stains, decades-old crumbs and sand between the leaves. But I will keep them forever. When people see the books in my house, the most common response is, 'Wow, have you read them all?' And I say yes, because it's mostly true. If they stay unread for a certain time, they're out.

What this goes back to is a kind of analogy for the Roman Catholic doctrine of transubstantiation. In the Catholic church, you do not eat the bread and drink the wine as symbols of Christ. You eat them because they are the *actual* body and blood of the saviour. The ritual turns bread and wine into something holy and substantial. I do not believe in priests' magic, but I do believe in mine. By digesting books, I am creating myself. You are what you read. This has nothing to do with writing, although it has been an essential precondition of becoming a writer. I would still be a reader if I'd never written a word, but I could never be a writer without having been a reader first. What passes for my inner life is to a great degree filled by those books on my shelves. They are, in some way, a material manifestation of myself, just like photo albums or certificates of achievement or a home or a handmade creation. If I had only read electronic books, I would have killed fewer trees and have consumed less petrol driving to shops and wasted less time in the eternal browse, but what would my life look like? It would be digitised, a virtual reality. I would need more imagination to see it, and I'm not sure that it's an imagination I have. Late at night, struggling to sleep, I would not be able to ghost around my shelves and say to myself – *Crime and Punishment* – sick on a friend's couch in New York when I was twenty-two; *Fear and Loathing in Las Vegas* – a riotous train trip up the north coast when I was nineteen; or *Invisible Cities* – suddenly figuring it out while sitting on a sand dune at Seal Rocks, I don't know how many years ago, but I can still feel that sand and smell the sea. They are my old friends, these books I have read, and they are here in my house with me, loyally, day and night, and unlike other friends they don't make a mess or empty out the fridge. *This Is Your Life* used to be presented as a book. This is my life, I think, standing in the dark before those spines.

I never said anything to the man on the plane. I was pretty mad at him for taking our lives in his hands. I was also resentful at the ebook itself for taking away that little piece of the puzzle from which I could construct, for that guy, an imaginary life, a personality, even perhaps a comrade. Instead of speaking, I looked down and lost myself in the one device that never had to be turned off, would never bring a plane down, or ever run out of battery power.

'I love that writing gives me the chance to create a space for reading: that somebody reading my book may later remember not only my words but the colour of the cover, the room they read it in, the rain that day, the sound of their grandmother sneezing, a tiger they saw sleeping at a zoo.'

Fiona McFarlane

I Will Tell You Something

Fiona McFarlane

READING IS A VERY STRANGE THING TO DO. I KNOW of no other activity that's so simple and so complicated all at once. On the face of it, it's simple to sit on your couch with an open book (unless you're very busy, as so many people seem to be; or prefer to read in bed; or tend only to read 30,000 feet in the air on your way to another country; or like listening to audiobooks through headphones that speak so far inside your ear it's as if the book is occurring in your brain – and it is – while you walk through the city, or run on a treadmill, or pull weeds from your garden). One of my favourite writers, Robert Walser, confessed that, 'When I read, I am a harmless, nice and quiet person and I don't do anything stupid'; this is part of the simplicity of reading, because it's true that while reading we're unlikely to be doing anything else, anything particularly harmful, unkind or noisy, and that's a great relief. Our limbs and heart and immune system aren't taxed by reading. Our eyes might be, but there are remedies for that: glasses, laser surgery, strong lighting, the lovely large print I see sometimes in library books that always looks as if it's been inked moments before by a tender hand.

I remember few things from the year I was four, but learning to read is one of them (I suspect this is true for most people). I recall the very specific feeling of unsurprised wonder as the alphabet resolved itself in my brain: *of course*, I thought, as if I was learning something I already knew, and I was a little in awe of it and of myself; this may have been the first time I ever thought consciously about my brain. (Now, when I travel in a foreign country that uses a different alphabet, I take pleasure in looking at words I can't begin to understand, because it's as close as I come to remembering what it was like not to be able to read.)

Aside from the eyes, it's the brain that makes reading complicated. So much is required of so many of its different parts. I'm delighted by research that shows which sections of the brain kindle and flare when we read poetry as opposed to prose, when we're required to tackle metaphor or process the grief that arises from the death of a fictional character. Thinking about what our brain does when we're reading is a little like going down the rabbit hole with Alice. How can it be capable of so much all at once? How can it conceive of the couch or the plane or the garden or the bed and at the same time an American presidency, an ancient war, a violent apocalypse, a different garden, a long, subtle party?

And it's not as simple as being in two worlds at once (as if that were simple). We exist in one world and create another by reading it (this is how it feels), but these worlds aren't separate. Our experience of reading *Anna Karenina* or *The Very Hungry Caterpillar* or *In Cold Blood* is different from anyone else's, because we bring our own world into the fictional one: there was that blonde girl at school called Anna, the bright, spitting caterpillars on the gumtrees in the garden, that film with an American farmhouse in it, the smell of frying garlic while we read chapter seven, the fact that we're eighteen, or thirty-eight, or seventy, and Japanese or Haitian or Swiss, and our mother once said to us in a certain tone of voice, 'Come inside now,' or we have no memory of our mother. Reading is so specific to the reader, which is one of the things I find exciting about writing.

Sometimes when I read, I try to watch my brain reading, which is very difficult to do. I might read a passage, then stop myself and think, *What did my brain just do? What does it see?* This is because I've recently read a book called *What We See When We Read*, by Peter Mendelsund. Mendelsund suggests that we only pretend to see things when we read, or that the vision generated when we read operates not on the principles of detail and exact replication, but connection and recognition and abstract lifelikeness. I like the idea that most of the time we don't see when we read, so much as recognise; and when we fail to recognise, something interesting happens. I have two favourite kinds of reading moments. The first are those in which I encounter something I didn't know I knew, and there's that sensation of unsurprised wonder all over again, which is shocking and vital and feels like a new, true way of seeing, which has only been waiting for its inevitable discovery. Patrick White's mad spinsters, for example. Alice Oswald's lists of the *Iliad* dead. The adjectives in *Moby-Dick*. What is my brain doing when it reads those? It's recognising itself, which is both a simple and a complicated thing for it to do.

My second favourite kind of reading moment comes when my brain is so surprised it's forced to stop and puzzle something out. Lately, I've been reading the fairytales compiled by the Brothers Grimm: all of them, not just 'Rapunzel' and 'Hänsel and Gretel' and 'Rumpelstiltskin', but lesser-known ones with wonderful titles like 'Lean Lisa', 'Donkey Cabbages' and 'Death's Messengers'. Very few fairytale characters do any reading, presumably because fairytales are originally an oral form; they speak to us out of a time when literacy was rare (but even their queens and wizards and wealthy merchants, whom you might expect to be literate, are too busy to read). I wonder what my childhood experience of fairytales would have been if I'd only heard them. My mother grew up with very few books; one of them was a Little Golden Book, *The Twelve Dancing Princesses*, which she treasured and kept and passed on to me. I loved the boldness of the soldier, the girls' obligation to dance, the snap of a twig from the diamond tree on the hidden staircase to the underground lake, the confusion of the youngest princess's oarsman when the invisible soldier stows away on her enchanted boat ('Why is the boat so heavy tonight, princess?'), the casual, haughty way in which the princesses condemn their suitors to death. For me, that story is inseparable not only from certain phrases in the Little Golden Book, but from the illustrations by Sheilah Beckett, who died in 2013 at the age of 100. Her images are vivid and crisp, sort of French-fairytale-medieval by way of the 1950s, and I loved them so much – and still do – that *The Twelve Dancing Princesses* is not just a Grimm fairytale (it's number 133 in their collection, and called 'The Shoes That Were Danced to Pieces') but a Sheilah Beckett fairytale. It's also the rubbed golden foil of the book's spine, its provenance as my mother's, the creak of the cardboard cover and the afternoon light on my grandparents' yellow-brown carpet. Surely I'd miss these things if I'd only ever heard the story spoken aloud? But I suppose I'd have other things, equally lovely: the teller's voice, the warmth of a fire, a sleepy, cosy fear of the winter dark. I love books as objects, I love my interaction with them, but I suspect that any important experience of story, any transforming act of the imagination will be memorable, both physically and emotionally, no matter the medium in which it arrives.

The edition of Grimm's tales I've been reading is also illustrated, by a man called Josef Scharl. Scharl was a German painter who died in the same year Sheilah Beckett's 'Princesses' was published. He was banned from painting by the Nazis and emigrated to America, where he illustrated the tales in a naïve, folkloric style: pen-and-ink images, resembling woodcuts, of castles, roses, slipper-wearing eagles, seven-headed dragons, and pigeons pecking out the eyes of traitorous princes. One of the strangest illustrations shows a lobster pursuing a hare – there's no lobster in the tale it accompanies, but there is a crab, and it is chasing a hare. This tale is called 'The Ditmars Tale of Wonders', and it's less than a page long. The first line is, 'I will tell you something.' The last line is, 'Open the window, that the lies may fly out.' What comes in between are some of the strangest words I've ever read, and it was while reading them that I realised the brain is best at catching itself reading when it's reading nonsense.

The second sentence of 'The Ditmars Tale of Wonders' is, 'I saw two roasted fowls flying; they flew quickly and had their breasts turned to heaven and their backs to hell, and an anvil and a mill-stone swam across the Rhine prettily, slowly, and gently, and a frog sat on the ice at Whitsuntide and ate a ploughshare.' This is nonsense on top of nonsense. If roasted fowls could fly, they wouldn't be upside down; if objects could swim, prettily or not, they wouldn't be heavy anvils and mill-stones; if there were ice at the height of summer, a frog wouldn't sit on it; nor would the frog be capable of eating a large, sharp blade. But it's precisely because these things are impossible that my brain seems to make an effort to imagine them. If the tale described a frog on a lily pad, I suppose I would accept a general impression of a frog on a lilypad; according to *What We See When We Read*, I wouldn't actually picture the frog on its pad, but, in its acceptance of something so expected, my brain would register frog and pad, and move on. Faced with the extraordinary, I find myself picturing the ice, the frog and the ploughshare; what's more, I attempt to make sense of the whole sentence by seeing all of its parts in the same image, so that the ice floats on the summer Rhine next to the anvil and mill-stone, which swim beneath the roasted fowl. I like thinking of the fowls' breasts browning in the sun. Simultaneously, because I know all of this to be nonsense, I'm thinking of a drowned anvil, melting ice, feathered birds, fly-eating frogs. This sentence allows me summer and winter at the same time; the birds are both roasted and unroasted; the anvil is heavy, and it also floats; the frog eats the ploughshare, and doesn't. The brain's capacity for contradiction is quite wonderful, and we call upon it all the time, particularly when we read. Nonsense like this makes obvious just how flexible our brain is, or can be; how equipped we are to conceive of opposites, and the pleasure we might feel in not being required to solve them.

This is why I love to read, and this is why I write. It's probably why I write fiction. I love reading, because it generates paradoxes we needn't try to reconcile. I love story, because it's a voice out of the winter dark. I love language, because it sets an anvil swimming 'prettily, slowly, and gently'. I love that writing gives me the chance to create a space for reading; that somebody reading my book may later remember not only my words but the colour of the cover, the room they read it in, the rain that day, the sound of their grandmother sneezing, a tiger they saw sleeping at a zoo. They might recognise these things, and at the same time encounter something improbably new. Writing gives me a chance to think inside an opposite, a paradox, a beautiful riddle, then share it with a person on their couch, in their plane seat, weeding their garden or running on a treadmill. It gives me the opportunity to say, to people I've never met, 'I will tell you something.' And this is why reading is so extraordinary. I open *Moby-Dick* and hear, 'I will tell you something.' I open *The Man Who Loved Children* and hear, 'I will tell you something.' It's remarkable, isn't it, that there is something to be told, and a book willing to tell it? Now open the window, that the lies may fly out.

'The act of literally spying out a book, picking it up, examining it, and wondering what this thing, this object, was. Why was one more attractive than another, both when you looked at it and then when you read it, even smelt it?'

Jill Jones

A Place of Possibilities

Jill Jones

READING FOR ME, AS A POET, IS ABOUT POSSIBILITIES. Because that is what my writing does, it deals with the many possibilities of language and meaning. For me, poetry begins in a space, the space of a page. And because you write with your body, writing comes from the body's space, and pace; its energy. The poems you read, the poems you write.

Poems also seem magical as words are magical. Sometimes, it's like a tuning in: you see or hear something and associate a word with it in the moment. It's an associative, or accretive process. And it goes or it doesn't. Hindsight can do the whys and wherefores, but the way we 'exist in language', to borrow a phrase from poet Nicole Brossard, is such a rich and momentary process that's hard to pin down.

I don't know when I decided I might be a poet. I'm not sure it's possible to pin down something like that. However, there are reading experiences that I am sure were the ones that showed me – not only showed me but pushed me towards that possibility.

The books I read as a child weren't chosen by me, of course. They were given to me as presents, they were school books, or they were books that were simply there, in the house. My early poetry reading experiences were not from books at home. They were the typical school experiences of class recitation from set texts, often of eighteenth- or nineteenth-century verse suitable for children, epic poems usually, or Australian bush ballads, with the occasional vaguely modern poem about something Australian, which still ended up being about 'the bush'.

The only specific poetry books I can recall from any of my family's bookshelves were books that belonged to my Scots grandmother. They were two grand, very weighty, dark-covered volumes with engraved illustrations: the collected poems of Robert Burns. Their spines were wrecked, the pages were foxed; they were quite old and in need of restoration, even back then. I still have them, still unrestored. As a child, I was more interested in how the books looked, rather than in reading Burns's verses, which I didn't really get, unsurprisingly.

In our house there were a number of books, mostly old, mostly hardback. Some of them were there before we moved in, left by a previous owner, and to a child these were strange, bookish books. In hindsight, I assume the house had been owned by someone connected to a university or to some Australian intellectual circle. I recall, though I have nothing tangible left with which to prove it, that at least one of the books had the name A. A. Phillips written on the flyleaf. The next-door neighbour's surname was Phillips. Was it a coincidence or did the owner of the house, or the next-door people, have some connection to the writer and critic A. A. Phillips, the man who coined the term 'cultural cringe' all the way down south in Melbourne? Who would know now? But I can still remember what the signature looked like.

The other books were my family's. We children often received books as gifts. I learnt to read and write fairly early. Books were there, to be looked at, to be handled, to be read. Most of the books in the house were kept on shelves at one end of a long, dark double room with dark green carpet, which we called the lounge room, though it was rarely used for lounging or for anything much, apart from the odd formal occasion.

The books I was given as a young child were simple illustrated stories or books about facts: on, say, dinosaurs or, my favourite, the solar system. From those early times, the story that affected me most, that scared me, was one about a family house burning down due to an electrical fault. At least, that's how I recollect it. I've been a bit iffy about electricity ever since. If it was supposed to be a cautionary tale – and what an odd kind of subject for a story, now I think about it – it worked.

The later childhood books I remember were mostly old, thick and musty-smelling volumes; for instance, Mary Grant Bruce's *Billabong* series (my mother's name was Norah) or *Anne of Green Gables*, *Seven Little Australians*, all of which I read, or *The Drums of Mer*, which I never actually read. Or classics such as *The Coral Island* by R. M. Ballantyne. When I think about it, they all seemed to be books about specific places with definite atmospheres. And not places nearby, not the mundane.

I would also read popular multi-volume illustrated encyclopaedias, simply dipping into pages that looked interesting – usually, but not always, with illustrations. These weren't expensive *Encyclopaedia Britannica* volumes but a series of books somehow acquired by my parents many years before I was born. Or the *Pears Cyclopaedia*, a one-volume staple in many houses then. They offered a collage of what the world might be, which appeared to consist of strange and unrelated facts and histories that might one day cohere into . . . something. I wasn't sure what the something might be, but the pick-and-mix approach was endlessly almost-satisfying. It was reading by chance, an associative process of gathering words and information. And these books always felt as though they carried weight and meaning of some kind. Dark red or brown colours, gold embossing. Importance.

At some stage a few volumes from the *Reader's Digest* 'Condensed' series of books appeared in the household. I never really read them, or only parts of one or two of them, but I recall they contained such works as Alan Paton's *Cry, the Beloved Country*, a title that intrigued me as a child, an idea of a place that was beloved. I had no idea of the novel's true import then, of course. In the same volume there was a condensed version of *The Cry and the Covenant*. All this crying. I wondered about that. I simply loved the board covers, their lovely patterns, and, again, the authoritative-looking spines.

When I was about eight years old, I tried to make a book, using a blank exercise book, coloured pencils, a pen of some kind and much drawing. It wasn't poetry and it was childlike, of course. But I have been interested in making things of words, on paper, in collections, ever since. I never finished that childhood book project but it made me wonder about what a book was, how you would make one. Perhaps, looking back, it showed me that a book is never finished.

I also read a lot of comics. My father worked in the advertising industry and had some business connection to magazine distributors Gordon and Gotch. So, for a time during my primary school years, he would bring home many different comics, though the bulk of them were DC Comics, featuring Superman, Batman, the Green Arrow and the further panoply of DC superheroes. Later, to my greater delight, there were copies of *Mad* magazine ('What, me worry?'). I'm not sure my mother ever entirely approved; for some reason comics were thought to be 'bad' for kids, but there they were, these bright, brash, exciting adventures, or clever takes on what, even then, I understood about politics and society. They seemed smarter and more up-to-date than the almost-required young girls' books, those little fictional women – the Norahs and Annes or Judys – plucky heroines, no doubt, but ever so slightly irrelevant to me.

A little while later in my childhood I was given an abridged prose version (it was in no way a translation) of the *Iliad* and the *Odyssey*. I realise now it was the version by Jane Werner Watson with splendid, vibrant and, for the times, modern-looking colour illustrations by Alice and Martin Provensen. It was a wonderful book to hold, and to behold. I wish I still had a copy. It was one of the first books I remember that I truly got lost in; a book of magic and marvellous things. In my mind, this is connected to having heard, a few years before, a retelling on the ABC radio of the Grail legend and the knights of the round table. So, an oral storytelling. To this day, I remember the hair standing up on the back of my neck as I listened, especially when Galahad reached his goal. This was mystery in words, in telling. I have no idea of the provenance of the radio series, whether it was even Australian in origin; it is the trace of the feeling that remains, that words make both mystery and enlightenment.

When I think back now, much of what I remember of a lot of this reading has to do with places, or particular things – the myths, legends and superhero comics were full of 'things' – or specific resonances. I have to admit I don't really recall a great deal of the plots of these stories and comics. To this day, plot both as a writer and as a reader often escapes me. When I was reading, I was in a world, not a plot. I responded to atmospheres, to places, the magic of them, transformations, of things and the non-human as well. Horses. Mirrors. Mountains. Seas. Trees. Lakes. Boats, both mystical and practical. Back then in childhood, it was anything but suburbia. A favourite book of my later childhood was called, if I remember correctly, *All About Archaeology*, and that took me to ancient Egypt, to Crete, to the diggings of Troy and thus the *Iliad* again. I think I even claimed to a school teacher that I wanted to be an archaeologist when I grew up. Gosh, all that digging! Even the girly books set in the bush or the outback were an escape. Somewhere else beyond Sydney rooms and streets. Somewhere 'real', even if it was an ancient real.

As may be obvious from all I've said, I was a child of the Australian suburbs, in Sydney's comfortable, middle-class North Shore, then, later, the northern beach suburbs: blank, sunny stretches that held nothing but boredom for certain kids, such as myself. Sure, there were still great tracts of semi-bushland to explore. I suspect we were much freer then to roam around, making up games and competitions in each other's houses, through the streets and areas not yet built upon, and there was fun in that. But I was a fairly serious child, not that interested in running and jumping competitions, not that physically adept, and fairly shy. I thought I had it figured out – that if I could get to a more complex adult world, things would be more interesting. I had determined in a childish form of logic that, essentially, there had better be more than this suburban existence, this Australian lassitude; otherwise, what was the point to anything and everything? All these books and stories and, okay, a bit of television, pointed to something more. It was a strange, dreamy kind of naivety.

However, despite all my fascination with the ways books looked and felt, and my love of reading (I was even scolded by the school librarian for reading 'beyond my age', though she did relent after quizzing me, and let me borrow books for 'older children'), I had no specific sense of being any kind of writer. My first school compositions, the ones that were supposed to be stories, were not very good. I even recall writing a story of the 'I woke and it was all a dream' kind, that quintessential creative-writing cliché. No, I wasn't good at plots. But I did like putting words together. However, I remember no poems I wrote, though I'm sure I did write some.

It was a little while longer, not until I reached my teens, when I had a further revelation through set school reading. I was studying English in second-year high school – Year 8, I guess it is now – and I recall we read these lines from Wordsworth's poem, 'Composed upon Westminster Bridge, September 3, 1802':

> This city now doth, like a garment, wear
> The beauty of the morning; silent, bare,
> Ships, towers, domes, theatres, and temples lie
> Open unto the fields, and to the sky

And I thought, wow, you could write about cities; it didn't have to be about gum trees, stockmen and kangaroos, or epics of ancient times or light brigades or ladies palely loitering. And it had a date in the title, it was very much of a specific time and place. Nowadays, of course, Wordsworth is considered somewhat reactionary, though he wrote that poem in his younger, radical phase, which many people tend to gloss over. Nonetheless, that discovery was all part of my experience as a reader and would-be writer. It had nothing to do with what my teacher may have thought she was teaching me, nor with what I know about Wordsworth and Romantic poetry now. It was a key moment of putting some things together in my head, about the possibilities of writing and also reading poetry. It was at this point I started to seek out some poetry books. They were mostly anthologies in the school library, but it was a beginning. It was also around the time I first discovered 'existentialism', my serious young insect phase, so I was haunting some of the less frequented library aisles.

Of course, my reading expanded even within the demands of the curriculum. What Australian high-school kid didn't read Kenneth Slessor back then? I'm surprised to find out how little younger readers and writers know of him, in fact – many of my own students have never even heard of him. But back then, poems such as 'William Street' and 'Five Bells' entered my consciousness. It's interesting to read Slessor's own notes on 'William Street' in the preface to his *Selected*. He says, 'The general reason for the poem remains, since it was intended as a defence of metropolitan fascinations against those who considered the city "ugly" and found beauty only in the outback.' The poem's first stanza, and its well-known refrain, reads:

The red globes of light, the liquor-green,
the pulsing arrows and the running fire
spilt on the stones, go deeper than a stream;
You find this ugly, I find it lovely

It may not be one of Slessor's best poems, in hindsight, but I'm thinking about beginnings, about what a kid embarking on reading and writing poetry might have thought possible. I was a very late beginner, in one sense, as it turned out.

As I got older, I 'escaped', to the supposedly more cosmopolitan, semi-bohemian inner city of Sydney. It was from there I started, eventually, to write. In my mind I was beginning with 'what I knew'. And that was my city, my suburbs. So, ironically, the suburban now offered itself as a subject, and as a real place at last. At the same time, I realised you could play around with language, as I found poets doing in anthologies of what was then called 'modern poetry', writing I finally discovered in my late teens. In other words, you could experiment. My first teenage experiments were forgettable, indeed dire, but at least some words got put down on paper.

So, I started writing this bad poetry, then stopped – that's another story – and didn't seriously get going till much later. However, I was continuing to look for books of poetry, and not simply the 'set' anthologies. It was hit or miss back then – literary books, poetry books weren't that easy to track down in Australia – but it was the beginning of a continuing search.

I still believe my various actual acts of reading in childhood were important, for myself as a reader and as a writer. The act of literally spying out a book, picking it up, examining it and wondering what this thing, this object, was. Why was one more attractive than another, both when you looked at it and then when you read it, even smelt it? This was a thing made of paper, cardboard, ink. Made of words and spaces, of typography and design.

Why was it special? It made you want to read it, and in that process it did something, if its charm worked. It was about possibilities, in, of, beside and through words. It was a place where things happened.

'It's always instructive to return to a book you admired a long time ago. It carries the ghost of the first reading.'

Joan London

The Only Russian in Sydney

Joan London

I FIRST READ *THE WATCH TOWER* BY ELIZABETH Harrower in the library of the University of Western Australia more than forty years ago. I must have found it while browsing the shelves of Australian fiction. I wasn't taking a course on Australian literature – there wasn't one. Even though I was enrolled in a course called The Modern Novel and was reading James Joyce and Ford Madox Ford – Virginia Woolf was the only female writer to merit a mention – I rarely read literary journals and had no real idea about the literary culture of my own country.

In spare moments I always ended up at the fiction shelves of the library, looking for books that would speak to me about my life and fate. I relied on random discoveries. *The Watch Tower*, published by Macmillan in London in 1966, would have been a relatively new acquisition.

The novel gripped me like a nightmare. It had the strong, lively, unflinching writing of someone with a story to tell, who goes deeper and deeper into the characters, their feelings and motives, as the narrative races along. Its scenes were vivid, of Sydney in the 1940s and 1950s with its bright air and glittering bays, and the house with the view, and the man who patrols it like an evil dwarf, rolling his eyes and rubbing his hands over some new way to torture his wife. *I didn't know* . . . I remember thinking that. I meant: I didn't know there was writing like this, in Australia, now, by a woman. I read it as if it were a thriller, obsessively, though no one is murdered. There is only, like the title of another great novel of psychological cruelty, the death of a heart.

The title itself had a contemporary resonance, provided by Bob Dylan's song 'All Along the Watchtower', released a year later: 'There must be some way out of here . . .'

For that is what the novel is about. Entrapment, and finding the way out. Or not.

The novel's opening line, 'Now that your father's gone . . .' has the ring of 'Once upon a time' in a fairytale, announcing an eternal theme in the history of storytelling, especially the novel: the fate of single women without a man in the family, or independent means.

Their selfish mother, more like a wicked stepmother, takes her two daughters, Laura and Clare, out of boarding school, to live with her in a flat in Sydney. Laura, the older by seven years, a promising student who wants to become a doctor, is sent to business college to learn shorthand and typing; and then, according to the rites of passage in those days, cuts off her plaits and becomes a secretary at a cardboard-box factory, for the enigmatic owner, Mr Felix Shaw. 'She had a sensation of having mislaid . . . a piece of herself. There was nothing to dream!'

World War II breaks out, and their mother leaves on the last ship home to England. Parentless, friendless, the sisters must move into a boarding house and fend for themselves. Sensitive, moral, intelligent, penniless girls, they are heroines worthy of Henry James, Jane Austen or Charlotte Brontë. To save Clare from leaving school at fourteen to work with her in Mr Shaw's next enterprise, a chocolate factory, Laura agrees to marry him.

> 'Mmm.' He moved his mouth ruminatively, never quite displacing that superior smile and its odd suggestion of complicity. Again he hummed out that long reflective noise. 'I don't know if we couldn't fix that up.'
>
> Laura was aware suddenly that her eyes felt strained and sore; the skin of her lips felt taut and cracked with the heat. Talking in this personal way to Mr Shaw made her feel nervous and giddy, or just peculiar and unlike herself.

Thus the elder sister, traditionally the surrogate mother, offers up her life for a home and security, and to give the younger a chance. Handed over by an unloving mother to a man unable to love, Laura has been groomed for victimhood. Because she is a principled person, she feels in debt to Mr Shaw. 'She had only herself, and out of herself she had somehow to manufacture repayments he would find acceptable.' How she toils! Chores abound in this mansion, as Laura, after a day in the office, scrubs and serves and weeds the garden, and won't ask for a penny for herself. A young woman in wealthy surroundings, she has faded dresses and worn hands.

Mr Shaw becomes Felix, 'a swarthy, nuggety man of forty-four . . . hardly taller than Laura in her two-inch heels . . . His voice grated and rasped as if his throat was perpetually rough from shouting.' He has a particular physical presence in the novel, his gestures and speech and 'his restless dark-brown eyes, the pores of his tough skin, his wrinkled sinewy throat and his, in some way, horribly incongruous, imported, impeccable clothes.'

Soon after the marriage he goes back on his word. Clare must leave school after all and go to business college. Endlessly, as if for sport, he invents ways in which to squeeze the joy out of Laura's life. He insists on Clare's constant presence too, 'to have her there to be knocked down, as it were, by the blows from his eyes and his words.'

Clare, a lover of Chekhov, Dostoyevsky and Tolstoy, isolated in that house, 'where there had never been a friend to call . . . only ever the indifferent, papery sound of wind in trees, distant traffic, winking planets', feels herself to be 'the only Russian in Sydney'.

I never forgot *The Watch Tower.* The vision of the book, the sense of darkness in sunlight, stayed lodged somewhere at the back of my mind. I remember the experience of reading it as intense, disturbing, though sometimes, in the sure hand of the creation of its villain, there was panache, even humour.

It's always instructive to return to a book you admired a long time ago. It carries the ghost of the first reading. Even though we now have words such as *misogyny* and *abuse* and *co-dependence* to name the forces that entrap the sisters, the tension is undiminished.

How a well-meaning young woman, brought up to be considerate of others, is harnessed to the demands of a damaged man is still excruciating to read four decades later. Who in the course of a life has not endured, or witnessed, or participated in the attempt of one human being to have power over another? Harrower's relentless observation of this process and its effects is worthy of the Russian masters.

'Little by little,' thinks Laura in a rare moment outside Felix's radar, 'she had resigned away the trust she had been given to be herself – out of pity, from a desire for peace at any price, thinking nothing really lost, anyway, by her silent acquiescence.'

To be herself. Unlike Laura, Clare has never signed away an inner life. Hers is the view from 'the watch tower', on guard for danger but also looking out at the world from a contemplative distance. *Reality.* That is her quest.

> This permanent awareness of what was so, regardless of her whims of the moment, regardless of what it would be pleasant to believe, or not pleasant, this solid bedrock was what she was, what she was about. What could there be in its place if you were differently constituted?

This awareness includes the acknowledgement of otherness, the respect for another's being. Sometimes there is joy, rapture, in light, or trees, or the humanness of strangers, but its practice is as austere as any other form of spiritual exercise.

What I had forgotten from my first reading, or perhaps was not ready to receive, is the strength of this slowly gathering counter-force, the means of resistance to the malevolence of Felix Shaw.

The assistance Clare offers Bernard, the young Dutchman, survivor of the war in Europe, is like the breaking of a spell. Suddenly she sees that 'she and Bernard had traversed the same extreme country'. It had never occurred to her that she could be useful to anyone. 'Yet she felt extraordinarily light-hearted – like a scientist at the very moment of discovery . . . There was boundless vitality of the spirit, a thoughtfulness beyond words. She could encourage someone to stay alive. And this was what she was for.'

Again and again Harrower defines the ways of the victims, the helpless. *The Watch Tower* is an extended study of suffering, whatever its origin. It is Bernard who has the last word on Laura as he watches her frantic search for the diamond ring that Felix has allowed her to believe she has lost.

> Laura had forgotten him, was unaware of his eyes on her, was so far removed from the light movement of the air, the scent of freesias, the shimmering of leaves, that she suddenly seemed to Bernard, who had seen many victims, to represent them all. She was unapproachable as the condemned are unapproachable and he was responsible, as the free always are.

Where does such knowledge come from? Each of Harrower's four novels is concerned with entrapment of one sort or another, through family or youth or love. But *The Watch Tower*, her last novel, is almost like a distillation in its vision of the forces of good and evil.

Something runs clear and strong through this wonderful, painful novel, the dark and the light. The victim and the survivor. Suffering and joy. The knowledge of both. *Reality.*

'A writer who says they don't read is akin to a swimmer who never jumps into a pool or won't invest in a pair of goggles.'

ANITA HEISS

Not All Writers Began As Readers

Anita Heiss

AS AN INDIGENOUS LITERACY DAY AND BOOKS IN Homes ambassador, *and* someone who completed a doctorate on Aboriginal literature and publishing, I am embarrassed to admit that I rarely read as a child in the 1970s. I remember sitting on my dad's lap and him reading me a Golden Book of some description when we still had black and white television. But other than that I am not one of those people who can glow with excitement recalling the books that had an impact on me in my youth.

I didn't read the entire Trixie Beldon collection like my friend Kerry did in primary school. I had to force myself to finish *What Katy Did* and *What Katy Did Next* in Year 6. And to be honest I couldn't tell you what they were about now. But perhaps 'Katy' did influence me, because from memory she was a tomboy, and so was I in many ways.

Like most of the kids (mainly boys) in the suburban street where I grew up, I spent my after-school hours and weekends in the early 1980s playing outside on the lawn and the then quiet road. We played cricket, footy, tennis and on really hot days in summer we'd roll out the slip 'n' slide. When we wanted to do something a little less energetic we generally spent a lot of time at number 11 because they had the best board games, a snooker table, and a kitchen in which we could all sit comfortably to play the card game UNO.

My youth was not like childhood today, when many kids are engaged by some form of technology – an iPad or iPhone, Wii, Nintendo, PlayStation and Xbox. Others I am around have their heads buried in books by Andy Griffiths, Jacqueline Harvey, John Green and so on. The competition with books in the old days was outdoor activities and group games. Times have certainly changed. We were a lot healthier back then too.

I'm pleased to say, though, that reading is still popular and I take my hat off to teacher-librarians for nurturing the love of reading in schools today. I walk into classrooms and school libraries when I do author talks and workshops and I ask students as young as seven what they like to read and who their favourite authors are. Often, especially with the primary-school kids, arms will shoot into the air immediately, with a passion and desperation to share their views and their favourite books. I read books as part of the MS Readathon, which started in Australia in the late 1970s, but I was *never* as excited about it as kids doing reading challenges are these days.

However, I *do* get excited about reading now. I found my true love of reading when I started my doctorate in 1996. I remember going to the Black Books shop housed at Tranby Aboriginal College in Glebe, and buying as many books by Aboriginal authors as I could: Ruby Langford Ginibi, Jackie Huggins, Lionel Fogarty, Kevin Gilbert, Jack Davis, Oodgeroo Noonuccal, Eve Fesl and Sally Morgan. My bookcases grew from that one visit and have continued to expand ever since.

Reading a diversity of Aboriginal voices across genres and across the country inspired me in my studies and in my eventual decision to become a writer. When I wrote my first book, *Sacred Cows*, I had no idea that I would become the author I am today. My reading of current Aboriginal novelists like Larissa Behrendt, Melissa Lucashenko, Alexis Wright, Kim Scott and Bruce Pascoe not only challenges my thought processes and supports my own world views but also motivates me to better my own craft. And that is why I believe writers need to read.

It was also while reading these writers that my attention was drawn to how important reading was in my life; at the same time, I became aware of how many of those in my world didn't read, and not always by choice. In the last decade I have become an advocate for increasing the awareness of literacy in Aboriginal communities because I want to see more of our mob reading. I would say that I was an ambassador for Aboriginal literacy before the official position was created with the establishment of the Indigenous Literacy Foundation (ILF).

Thanks to the wonderful Suzy Wilson, Australian of the Year for Queensland in 2014, and owner of Riverbend Books in Brisbane, the ILF was established as a cross-industry, grassroots movement and charity to ensure kids in remote communities have access to books and the joy reading brings so many of us, including you reading this anthology.

Suzy's question to all who will listen is, 'Can you imagine a world without books?' And most of the people in her world, and mine, can't imagine not having access to books, let alone not being able to read them. So with that in mind, it wasn't a difficult task to get a groundswell of support from the publishing and bookselling community, including authors and illustrators, to set up what has now been recognised internationally for its work: in 2014 the ILF was awarded the prestigious International Education Initiatives Award, announced at the London Book Fair.

The role and necessity of reading in every Australian's life, and the appalling statistics attached to Indigenous peoples in remote communities, are the driving forces for the volunteers and donations that form the basis of the ILF and its success. As an ambassador I am just one of many authors – Kate Grenville, David Malouf, Samuel Wagan Watson, Alexis Wright, Tara June Winch – who want Indigenous kids in remote communities to have the same opportunities as other Australian kids when it comes to the benefits that literacy in the English language can bring. Since the ILF became a foundation in 2011 it has raised over $2 million, delivered over 65,000 books to children in remote Indigenous communities, published and funded in partnerships thirty-seven community literacy projects, and launched an early literacy project, Book Buzz, in a number of communities.

My passion and concern are not simply because I am an author, though. As a Wiradjuri woman who has access to books in the city via the schools I attended and the wonderful local libraries in the Randwick municipality, I recognise I am privileged simply because I have had all the benefits that being literate can bring. Literacy has afforded me a postgraduate education and employment in many sectors of my own choice. Literacy has given me the self-determination that those who can't read lack. Those without literacy often cannot make everyday decisions for themselves because they don't have the basic skills to do so. That means they are constantly relying on other people – often non-Indigenous people – to make decisions for them. That is not Aboriginal self-determination in my eyes.

Being illiterate – not being able to read books, newspapers, websites, street signs, health information, safety warnings and personal correspondence – is a major barrier to education, employment, health and wellbeing. Some of the more disturbing of the statistical facts related to this issue include the following: by the age of twelve, approximately 85 per cent of Indigenous children in remote and isolated areas are unable to read at the minimum level; by the age of fifteen, more than a third of Australia's Indigenous students do not have literacy skills good enough to allow them to meet real life challenges.

The most recent data shows there is an enormous gap in literacy rates for Indigenous people living in remote communities, and it emerges at an early age. Non-Indigenous students far outperform Indigenous students in benchmark tests for reading, writing and numeracy in Years 3 and 5. By Year 7, the gap has widened. In the Northern Territory only one in five children living in very remote Indigenous communities can read at the accepted minimum standard. By Year 7, just 15 per cent achieved this benchmark, 47 percentage points behind their urban Indigenous peers and 74 per cent less than non-Indigenous students.

What these statistics tell me is that these kids – in all likelihood – will go on to become adults solely reliant on non-Indigenous people to make decisions for them in key areas of their lives. This is the opposite of self-determination for Indigenous people. This is why it's important for us to continue to support this project and raise awareness however we can.

Back in 2011, when I heard about the BBC Book Challenge listing 100 books, it was claimed that most people had only read six of the 100. When I first read the list, I wondered what an Indigenous list might look like, and how much home-grown Indigenous literature most Australians would have read. I had previously been asked for recommendations of titles and authors, so I thought it was time to put together a list of my favourite Indigenous-authored books across genres: fiction, non-fiction, poetry, children's, published plays and anthologies. The list was by no means definitive: there are more than 5000 published Aboriginal and Torres Strait Islanders in Australia indexed into the BlackWords database of AustLit. To make it easy I simply scanned my shelves at home and made a list of some of my 'must reads', which I posted on my blog as recommended reads. Many of the authors I listed had published works across genres, but I limited myself to one book per author. I chose to list only 99 titles and left the 100th to my blog visitors.

I ordered my list by title and then waited for the overwhelming response. I'm told libraries around the country use the list to stock their shelves and recommend titles to their visitors. The list has been so popular that I had to generate a new one in 2013 of another 99 titles – this time with genres noted next to each title.

Times have indeed changed since I was a street-cricket-playing-tomboy-who-didn't-read. In 2012 I was an ambassador for the National Year of Reading. That's right. Me, Anita Heiss – who managed to get through some subjects in her undergraduate degree by only reading indexes of books – was asked to spend twelve months promoting the love of reading. I decided that as part of my ambassadorship I would set a personal challenge of reading 52 books in 52 weeks. It was an ambitious challenge for me as I am a slow reader, a very slow reader, and I am happy to be a slow reader, because as a writer, I want my own readers to take in e-v-e-r-y s-i-n-g-l-e word. And so I took to reading with a sense of purpose and a goal to be reached. The authors I took with me to bed, to the beach, on flights and in the bath that year included: Alice Pung, Nicole Watson, Charlotte Wood, Kylie Ladd, Lisa Heidke, Emily Maguire and Amal Awad. A good dose of Aussie women writers there! I also read a number of fabulous children's books published by One Day Hill press in Melbourne.

In 2014, I gave myself the same challenge as one of my New Year's resolutions. My list of authors and their books had an international slant, with Alice Walker, Toni Morrison, John Green and Chimamanda Ngozi Adichie. I also read a lot of the newer titles in the Yarning Strong series of Aboriginal stories for primary school readers. Yes, I know these are easy reads, but as I emphasised in the National Year of Reading 2012 – all reading matters!

My latest novel, *Tiddas*, is centred around a group of friends in a book club. I chose the book club because I wanted to be able to write into my own novels the books that I think all Australians should read. They are books by both Aboriginal and non-Aboriginal authors that have touched me in some way, and, importantly, include this country's First Nations people within their stories. Books like Chloe Hooper's *The Tall Man*, framed around the tragic death of Cameron Doomadgee in police custody in 2004. This book not only tells the story of Palm Island, its history as a mission, an 'open-air jail' and forgotten community, but, most importantly, is a heart-wrenching example of the deathly flaws of the policing system in Queensland and nationally. It brought me to tears. That's the power of the writing, and the experience of reading.

I want to feel something when I read. I want to be transported to places throughout time, and I want to see Australia's political, cultural and social landscape on the page. I want to read about women like myself, as well. I want my reading experience to be authentic, and as a writer, I want to know the author has researched the story, the setting, and the characters and portrayed an authentic account of their topic. Terri Janke's *Butterfly Song*, for example, is a love story, a crime novel, a lesson in native title and it informs the reader about some of the culture and history of the Torres Strait. It is also funny. I have read that book a number of times because I like the way it makes me feel.

Tiddas is set in Brisbane, so it was also important for me to include Nicole Watson's *The Boundary* on the book-club reading list because it's set in West End and talks about the history of the invisible boundary that Aboriginal people couldn't cross to go into the city. Everyone in South Brisbane at the very least should know about it.

I teach creative-writing workshops in schools and through writers' centres. I tell my students they cannot expect to be writers if they do not read. Reading is our homework, if you like. We need to read to better understand our own voice on the page, to actually create a voice we like for ourselves and our characters, and we need to read widely across genre, gender, geography and cultures. If we are writing to be published, we need to read to understand the marketplace and what our competition is. You can't sell a story that's already been told in ten different ways. Writers need to read to know where the gap in the market is. I tell my students to create their own niche, but in order to know what it is, they need to know what hasn't been created yet.

A writer who says they don't read is akin to a swimmer who never jumps into a pool or won't invest in a pair of goggles. A dancer who doesn't stretch. A runner who doesn't understand the role of protein and carbohydrates in their diet. It is impossible to be a half-decent writer if you don't read. I tell my students in classrooms around the country that even though I didn't read as a child, as an adult I love reading and the places it takes me, the wisdoms it gives me, the peacefulness it instils in me, the emotions it evokes in me, and the companionship a good book offers me at any hour of the day. A friend gave me a gift a few years back. It's a wooden sign you hang in your home. It rested in my bedroom for a while, it now sits on my bookshelf in another room. It says: 'Book lovers never go to bed alone!'

If I were to make a sign, I'd write: 'If you have a book, you will never be alone!'

'It is as if you had discovered the key not just to a book but to the world – a world full of signs to be read, and interconnections you had not previously imagined.'

DAVID MALOUF

Reading the Signs

David Malouf

THERE ARE SOME BOOKS THAT MAKE SUCH A VIVID impression on us, put us so deeply under their spell, that our first acquaintance with them becomes a watershed in our lives, and the actual reading – the excited turning of pages over a period of hours or days – seems in retrospect to have taken place in a country all its own, with a light and weather like no other we have ever known.

I read *Jane Eyre* in the Christmas holidays – the long summer break – between primary and secondary school; I was not quite thirteen. Some of it I read slumped in a canvas chair on our beach-house verandah, within sound of the surf; some of it on the beach between swims. What extraordinary creatures we are that we can be, on the same occasion, in two quite different places; and what a business reading is that fifty years after the event the landscape of Thornfield in the frost, as I first came upon it, is as present in my memory as the hot sands of Main Beach, Southport and my own body under the blazing sun. What did I get from the book that it should have hit so hard?

The voice of the narrator, first of all, which, once you have given yourself up to it, is irresistible; so close, so much part of your own inner world that everything Jane sees and feels is immediately a revelation. It is as if you had discovered the key not just to a book but to the world – a world full of signs to be read, and interconnections you had not previously imagined.

One of those interconnections is between individuals. Ardently romantic, the announcement of it comes to the adolescent of either sex as a lightning flash.

'He is not of their kind,' Jane tells herself of Mr Rochester, rejecting at a stroke all the circumstances that divide them. 'I believe he is of mine – I am sure he is – I feel akin to him – I understand the language of his countenance and movements: though rank and wealth sever us widely, I have something in my brain and heart, in my blood and nerves, that assimilates me mentally to him.'

Rousing stuff, this bold assertion of the primacy of feeling, this sympathy between souls that can leap across real space as well as social barriers, and is grounded in the physical but can so immediately transcend it. Jane is not even in solitude when she hears the voice of Mr Rochester calling to her out of the night.

> The one candle was dying out: the room was full of moonlight. My heart beat fast and thick: I heard its throb. Suddenly it stood still to an inexpressible feeling that filled it through, and passed at once to my head and extremities. The feeling was not like an electric shock, but it was quite as sharp, as strange, as startling: it acted on my senses as if their utmost activity hitherto had been but torpor, from which they were now summoned and forced to wake. They rose expectant: eye and ear waited, while the flesh quivered on my bones.

One of the things that convinces us most in this passage is that in describing the state in which Mr Rochester's voice comes to her, the words Jane finds, in their rhythm, in the intensity with which the physical and the mental become one, reproduce just the state in which Jane's voice, as narrator, comes to us. We believe utterly in the form of sympathy she proposes because we ourselves are the subject of it.

Late in the book, Jane pictures the world for us as a network of such correspondences or sympathies – between individual souls, between individuals and what they produce – her pictures, for example, which Mr Rochester takes as clues to her inner world – between events in the human sphere and their reflection in Nature. Interpreting the world is a matter of reading 'signs'. 'Presentiments are strange things!' Jane tells us. 'And so are sympathies; and so are signs: and the three combined make one mystery of which humanity has not yet found the key.'

As for the tale she has to tell, Jane is so sympathetically attuned to the events of it that they seem at times to be no more than a projection of her own intimate yearning. She stands, as a narrator, somewhere between Catherine Morland of Jane Austen's *Northanger Abbey*, whose thinking is so conditioned by the sensational novels she has absorbed that she mistakes the oddness of people, and the strangeness of real life, for the making of yet another Gothic fiction, and that other governess and servant of an absent master, the anonymous narrator of Henry James's *The Turn of the Screw* – 'young, untried, nervous' – whose account of the 'mysteries' at Bly hovers so ambiguously on the edge of neurotic fantasy.

There is no ambiguity in Jane's case. In her down-to-earth way, she resists the suggestion that Thornfield may house a mystery. But the world of story – 'Passages of love and adventure taken from old fairy tales and other ballads or (as at a later period I discovered, from *Pamela*)' – has a strong influence on what she has to tell.

Writing of her free hours, she tells us:

> The restlessness was in my nature . . . Then my sole relief was to walk along the corridor of the third storey, backwards and forwards, safe in the silence and solitude of the spot, and allow my mind's eye

> to dwell on whatever bright visions rose before it . . . and, best of all, to open my inward ear to a tale that was never ended – a tale my imagination created, and narrated continuously; quickened with all of incident, life, fire, feeling, that I desired and had not in my actual existence.

The place Jane chooses for her reveries, the corridor of the third storey, is itself significant, though she does not as yet know it. 'One would almost say,' Mrs Fairfax tells her, 'that, if there were a ghost at Thornfield Hall, this would be its haunt.'

There is no ghost, but Jane, with her usual prescience, does see something. 'With its two rows of small black doors all shut,' it is 'like a corridor in some Bluebeard's castle'. When, later, she sits alone at dusk on the stile in Hay Lane and hears the approach of hooves, 'all sorts of fancies', she tells us, 'bright and dark tenanted my mind: the memories of nursery stories were there amongst other rubbish'.

The sturdy common sense of that 'amongst other rubbish' speaks for the side of Jane's nature that is suspicious of mysteries and of the irrational. The dash of cold water it provides (quite literally and comically in the case of Mr Rochester's bed) is meant to save her from falling into Catherine Morland's error; whereas it is only by accepting the irrational, and making a place for the extreme, that she might have discovered, behind Grace Poole with her 'pot of porter', the even darker figure of Mrs Rochester. She even misreads the events in Hay Lane. 'The incident had occurred and was gone for me: it was an incident of no moment, no romance, no interest in a sense.'

This is plain Jane speaking. Closer to the truth is the Jane who, just before the appearance of her phantom rider, remembers 'certain of Bessie's tales wherein figured a North-of-England spirit . . . which, in the form of a horse, mule, or large dog, haunted solitary ways . . .'

This spirit first takes the form of a dog, Mr Rochester's mastiff, Pilot, then of a horse and rider, and though 'The man, the human being, broke the spell at once,' her apparition, her demon lover, continues to inhabit a form halfway between animal and human. When a voice tells her to stand aside, 'I did,' she says, 'whereupon began a heaving, stamping, clattering process, accompanied by a barking and baying.'

The spell of Bessie's tale is not quite broken, and it is part of the erotic power of Jane's narrative that Mr Rochester continues to carry into later episodes a hint, in Jane's mind as in ours, of the Beast of fairytale and folk story who must be transformed back into a man.

She first discovers Mr Rochester's presence at Thornfield by finding his surrogate, Pilot, on the sitting-room rug, and it is, as she later tells him, not a philtre but the magic of a 'loving eye' that makes him 'human' again, though it is part of the book's tenacious hold on reality that Jane is no Beauty, and Mr Rochester no Prince. 'I had hardly ever seen a handsome youth,' she tells us at her first sight of him, 'never in my life spoken to one. I had a theoretical reverence and homage for beauty, elegance, gallantry, fascination; but had I met those qualities incarnate in masculine shape, I should have known instinctively that they neither had, nor could have sympathy for anything in me.'

There it is again: 'sympathy'. Jane – plain-looking, plain-spoken, 'original'; no more a conventionally attractive young woman than she was, to her aunt, a conventionally acceptable child – is perfectly fitted to this ugly, cross-grained man, whose 'savage' nature disguises surprising gentleness.

With no previous experience to go on she hits immediately on the style of flirtation by which he may be caught, so that when, at the end of their first conversation, the word 'coquetry' drops into the text – in relation to Adèle's perfectly conventional little imitation of it – we have confirmed what we have already understood: that Jane's refusal to play the submissive Victorian maiden, even to a man who is paying her thirty pounds a year, is her own form of coquetry, and the most effective form of it she could have hit upon.

What she does not see is that in failing to present him with a 'ladylike submission and turtledove sensitivity', in answering back so boldly, and allowing him to speak to her of his 'opera mistresses', she has led Mr Rochester to believe that she may also be willing to *act* unconventionally. He is looking for a woman who will follow him in intentions 'that require a new stature to legalise them', and this of course Jane will not do.

Meanwhile, any haunting that takes place in the book is by the ghosts these lovers find in one another.

He pretends to believe that it is a faery child he has found on the stile in Hay Lane, and when she comes back from Gateshead and confesses that she has been with her aunt, 'who is dead', Mr Rochester replies playfully, 'Good angels be my guard. She comes from another world . . . If I dared, I'd touch you, to see if you are of substance or shadow, you elf!' (Only a moment earlier, when she came upon him, Jane's first thought had been, 'Well, he is not a ghost; yet every nerve I have is unstrung.')

When later they sit alone at supper together, she tells him, 'You, sir, are the most phantom-like of all: you are a mere dream.'

Dreams, premonitions, sympathies, signs . . .

Jane draws the portrait of her rival and anti-self, Blanche Ingram, before she has even laid eyes on her; she sees in a dream the burnt-out shell of Thornfield; 'Bride' is one of the clues, and 'Bridewell' (prison) the solution in the game of charades Mr Rochester's guests engage in after dinner, but Jane's attention is elsewhere and she misses what all this might reveal to her of the larger mystery. The moth that catches Mr Rochester's eye in the Eden-like orchard on Midsummer's Eve, where he proposes to Jane, is like 'a West Indian insect', and the chestnut tree under which they make their vows, in a sudden shift of the weather, is struck by lightning, though the riven trunk, as Jane later discovers, still has shoots of green.

These 'signs' either enlighten Jane or mislead her, according to whether she follows one side or the other of her nature. They are also signs that we must interpret as readers, part of the book's brilliantly controlled suspense. But the deeper source of our suspense is the concern we feel for Jane herself.

Charlotte Brontë places Jane at the extreme edge of the social world. Orphaned and dependent, she is 'less than a servant' at Gateshead because she does nothing for her keep, and, as a governess, as Charlotte Brontë knew from bitter experience, she is in the anomalous position at Thornfield of being both a paid servant and a 'lady'. All this makes Jane acutely sensitive to every sort of injustice.

'Unjust – unjust!' she cries in the first pages of the book, and it is typical of her that she should speak out both for Blanche Ingram and Bertha Rochester when she believes Mr Rochester has failed to consider their feelings or their rights.

In the most extreme of the book's moves after her flight from Thornfield, Jane falls out of the safe net of society into that homeless and unsettled space between houses that is the abode of Wordsworth's beggars and of vagrant women like Alice Brown in *Dombey and Son*. She is saved by a couple of narrative ploys that belong to an altogether inferior sort of fiction, but Brontë recovers, and so does Jane. Faced with a subtle temptation to become conventionally submissive, she resists 'the flame and excitement of self-sacrifice', and with her old 'un-feminine' candour tells St John Rivers, that embodiment of genuine Christian virtue and soft male tyranny, 'If I were to marry you, you would kill me. You are killing me now.'

What saves her is not only the strong sense of her own worth, but also her experience of what love really is.

'He pressed his hand firmer on my head, as if he claimed me,' she writes of Rivers; 'he surrounded me with his arm, almost as if he loved me (I say almost – I knew the difference – for I had felt what it was to be loved . . .).'

After one hundred and fifty years this speaks as plainly and as directly to the reader as when it was written, and powerfully addresses – even now, when relations between women and men are more open and equal – questions about true feeling and the use of power that have still, in every case, to be negotiated.

No other Victorian novel, not even *David Copperfield*, presents us with a childhood and schooldays more fully realised. No death bed in Victorian literature is seen with a truer and less sentimental eye than that of Aunt Reed. No other novel in the language has produced so many offspring: from *The Turn of the Screw* ('was there a "secret" at Bly . . . an unmentionable relative kept in unsuspected confinement?'), to Jean Rhys's *Wide Sargasso Sea* or Daphne du Maurier's *Rebecca*.

Somewhere on a scorching beach, or tucked up in a sickbed, a new reader, for whom this book is just what they have been waiting for, is about to begin the first sentence of what will be one of the great reading experiences of their life. 'There was no possibility of taking a walk that day.' Their whole world is about to change.

'Reading is a kind of waking dream, where we can believe the magic is real, in a way we know it can never be in real life.'

SUNIL BADAMI

In Your Dreams

Sunil Badami

'A book is a dream that you hold in your hands.' Neil Gaiman

I'VE CONSIDERED MYSELF A READER FOR AS LONG AS I can remember, long before I ever dared admit I was a writer. I was always reading as a child, and I'd read anything: the cereal box over breakfast; the newspaper, wiped of dew; the school bulletin board; whatever my eyes fell on in the library during lunch; the labels on all the medications I had to take; the tattered old gossip magazines in my mother's surgery waiting room while we waited for her to finish the evening consultation – even the medical journals she kept in the staffroom. At night, I had to read before I went to sleep, and often well past bedtime, the shadows dancing over my bedroom wall.

According to my mother in an oft-repeated story, now oft-repeated to my children, when we went to an especially sacred temple in India, in which the gods would bestow any boon you wished for, while my brother asked for toys, I asked for books, books and more books.

Yet ours wasn't a family that read – any more than it talked. My parents' bookshelves were sparsely stocked, and I can't remember my mother ever reading a book; my father took over ten years *not* to finish a book about Ota Benga, the pygmy caged at Bronx Zoo. I don't remember either of them ever reading to us as children.

I was always in trouble for reading when I should have been doing whatever it was I was meant to be doing. 'Get your head out of that book and do something *useful*,' my father would say. 'Stop being so dreamy and focus on real life.'

But what was real life anyway? Constantly being reminded how useless and pointless I was at home, or how black and weird I was at school? I was always being asked where I was *really* from, and I never quite fitted in wherever I was. Although I was made to feel guilty that I wasn't out in the 'fresh air', it never discouraged me – if anything, the opposite. I remember long, dreamy afternoons of reading and re-reading *The Reader's Digest Book of Strange Stories, Amazing Facts*, Little Golden Books about saggy, baggy elephants, and Ladybird books about heroes like Clive of India, who conquered the wicked Indians – although in the *Amar Chitra Katha* comics all Indian children my generation grew up with, the English were cruel and cartoonishly pink.

The first long, non-picture book I ever remember reading was an old Ashton Scholastic school book-club life of Louis Braille. I was six, and read it in one afternoon, lying on the vinyl couch in our old house.

I'd never liked reading before that; I can remember what trouble my brother and I got into for tearing the pages out of an omnibus volume of Golden Books (which my daughters now have, though I still feel ashamed when I see it on the bookshelf, the sticky-taped scars a reminder). And I can remember my mother trying to teach me to read *The Jungle Book*, and my frustration at not being able to make sense of the words.

But as I read Louis Braille's story in that book without pictures, I felt like one of those blind people finally able to read, thanks to his invention, seeing something I couldn't have imagined before. I suppose you could say I never really looked back after that.

Although Graham Greene noted in his memoir, *Ways of Escape*, that the writer's childhood is his bank account – and, as a writer, it's probably the only bank account I've never been overdrawn on – I've forgotten most of mine: only impressions remain, even if those that do are vivid and visceral.

Like the stories my mother used to tell us of India, so magical and so far away, my childhood memories have always felt somewhat apocryphal, fictional, somehow second hand or made up, so I can't be sure if the memory is mine, or my mother's, as though what I think I remember is really what I remember of one of the few pictures taken of me as a child, or just another story she told me. (But don't take my word for it – I was a terrible fibber as a child, something both my parents swore I got from the other.)

I *do* remember how my nights as a child were filled with the sound of my parents fighting, and torrid recurring nightmares the year my father finally left. When the worst two or three of those dreams return, I'm a child again, and the shivering traces of the nightmares are as real as any uncertain childhood memories. In all of them, I'm lost, looking for a way of escape.

But in the same way that I've forgotten much of my childhood and nearly all of my dreams, I can't really remember many of the books I've read, especially some I loved the most. Then again, I can't remember the names or faces of many people I once loved the most either.

As Siegfried Sassoon once said, 'It is humanly certain that most of us remember very little of what we've read. To open almost any book a second time is to be reminded that we had forgotten well-nigh everything that the writer told us. Parting from the narrator and his narrative, we retain only a fading impression . . .'

Doesn't that happen with dreams? Terrified or elated beyond belief – and then, on waking, unable to recall anything. And if none of it happened, why do we *feel* as if it somehow did, and in a way more real than anything in our waking life that may have happened, but which we can't for the life of us remember at all? It makes me wonder why, if we forget most of what we read, do we read at all?

According to my mother, I was a solitary, singular child, whose only friend was imaginary. But neither of us can remember her name, and I couldn't tell you what she looked like now. Who said misery loves company? With no friends – my imaginary one long since gone and forgotten by the time I reached school – I found refuge at lunchtime, and recess, and after school, in the library. Books were a way of escape: and back then I read fantasies – titles that come to mind like *The Lion, the Witch and the Wardrobe*, *The Hobbit*, *The Wolves of Willoughby Chase* – in which all the characters were outcasts, outsiders, orphans, odd-bods, all as misunderstood and unbelieved and lost and lonely as I was. I followed them through the wardrobe door and the woods and the Mines of Moria, looking for treasures beyond words.

For years, I read books for the same sense of accomplishment as completing that same kind of magical quest, where everything was unimaginably exciting, and far away from wherever I was, where I could imagine I was anyone else but me.

The inescapable irony of reading and writing is that they are essentially solitary activities. I'm all too aware of that, isolating myself from the people I love, to write about people who don't exist, so that people I may never meet can isolate themselves from the people they love, to read about them. Unlike a singer or dancer, who can see and hear their audience, writers and readers are as separated by their isolations as they are connected by them – alone, apart *and* together. As Rebecca Solnit says, 'Living in books is an act that is so intimate and yet so alone . . . is the shared solitude of writing that separately we all reside in a place deeper than society, even the society of two?'

Perhaps. It might also be why I don't much care for book readings or audio books. Nobody's voice – even the author's – can sound like that voice in your head. (The *only* exception being when a soft, drowsy little leg is draped over you, and you're reading with your children. But that's another bedtime story.)

When my wife and I are in bed, in that sweet, quiet time before sleep, there's nothing guaranteed to evoke more viscerally the loneliness of the long-distance runner than either of us reading out a bit we love from our book. And heaven help me if I try to recount the dream that woke her up with my kicking and moaning! Dreams, unlike books, mean even less to anyone but the dreamer (which is why I skip dream sequences in novels).

I think it was Helen Garner who wrote something about her dream journal – was it in her collection *True Stories*? – about how you had to write the dream down the moment you woke up, before you even had time to think about it. The moment you *did* try to think about it, language forced a narrative upon it, and once that happened, the dream would be lost. The essence was the *feeling*, which, when I think about it, describes the sum of most of the books I've read, and much of my life.

All we have left from most of the books we've ever read or what life we've lived is a series of half-remembered moments and feelings; although life is like a dream in that it's a series of discrete, disparate, chance events – books we've forgotten and the memories of our lives are strung together with narrative, itself a kind of fiction, omitting this, confabulating that.

Like the memories you can't be sure aren't just memories of pictures, or memories of your dreams themselves, what you imagine and what you remember blur into each other, just like dreams and life and fact and fiction do. Paul Auster once said that he was halfway through *Pride and Prejudice* before he realised all the action was taking place in his parents' front room in New Jersey. I know many of the books I read until I was well into my twenties took place in the cold, dark, echoing hallways of school and the house my parents shared before my father left – just as many of my dreams did. Perhaps that's why seeing the adaptation of a book, especially one you love, can be so disappointing. The best books are like journeys to another country, full of sights and sounds, digressions and false trails, shouts and whispers, unspoken moments and entire lives. When all this is shoehorned into two or three hours – or worse, entirely changed so that it's nothing like your memory of the book – it feels as if someone has stolen or tarnished a precious memory. And the characters, whom you've grown to know and love as intensely as fellow travellers in another country, don't look or sound how you imagined them. Not that a precise description is any help either, and I instinctively resile from any, like the description of the protagonist in *The Da Vinci Code*, which I flung away as soon as I read some ridiculous line about 'Harrison Ford in Harris tweed' (and it makes you wonder if they changed the film tie-in to 'Tom Hanks in Harris tweed').

As I read, my image of the characters, especially the protagonist, shifts as details whinny through: hair colour and height change, the arch of an eyebrow means something else, the shadows and light shift and fade, just as they do in dreams, as though the hero really does have a thousand faces. While I couldn't draw you a picture of them, I know in my heart what they *should* look like, just as I do anyone I once knew or loved, like my imaginary friend, or real long-lost friends and former lovers, reduced to vague descriptions and gestures, as their faces and voices have faded from my memory. What's worse is that the actors, most of whom you recognise already, only seem to be *playing* the characters, rather than *inhabiting* them as you did reading their story; and if you ever re-read the book after seeing the adaptation, what you imagined is lost, replaced by what you saw.

There's a power to seeing something you can't actually see: the visions of prophets, as they are written and unseen by the eye, seem all the truer for that, just like dreams sometimes do too. Reading is a kind of waking dream, where we can believe the magic is real, in a way we know it can never be in real life.

Imagination and memory are the same, seeing what you cannot actually see. Some might say that the memories we have of particular novels and the deep feelings for characters in them are as false as any dream memory or imaginary friend, but as I get older, I'm finding with my own memories and children, memory itself is a kind of secret fiction, always changing: the stories we tell ourselves – and our children – as fictional as the stories our parents ever told us. What *did* the blind Jorge Luis Borges see when he imagined that Library of Babel, wandering its labyrinthine rooms, searching for meaning in that invisible line from room to room, book to book?

E. M. Forster famously called for literature not to be a sermon, and like him I don't believe in treating books as some kind of holy relic (although my mother always impressed on me that because Saraswati, the goddess of knowledge, lived in every book, you couldn't touch one with your foot, a rule I still enforce with my own bemused children). And I'm still not dogmatic about what I read or how I read it. I'm as happy to read on the Kindle as I am opening an old first edition, the previous owner's name inscribed on the frontispiece. Each has its own pleasures and limitations. It just has to be *good*: you won't love it any more because it's leather-bound or won a prize.

But, looking back, I'm struck by how my reading has changed over the years. Not just technologically – after all, is there any more obsolete medium than a book, which, at least in comparison to mobile phones, hasn't changed in hundreds of years, and which is essentially words on a page that mean nothing unless you can read them and understand them?

For years I read for accomplishment – books I thought I should read – and escape – books I knew I wasn't meant to. I struggled with *Ulysses* and *Moby-Dick* or whatever was that year's forgettable Miles Franklin or Booker Prize winner, feeling like a failure because I couldn't understand them or enjoy them, just as writing essays at school about the symbolism in *Of Mice and Men* or what the Dickens the author may have intended in *Great Expectations* seemed to stamp out the magic – especially the dark, ineluctable, irresistible magic of reading something you knew you shouldn't.

Once, throwing aside another forgettable book I couldn't bring myself to finish, it struck me that reading mightn't so much be a vocation of appreciation, but a calling of disappointment, in which you didn't so much kill the thing you love, but the love of it. The more books you read, the more bad ones you read too, the more eventually you feel less of the *art* and see more of the *craft*; the more you see the imperfections, the implausibilities, the impediments to enjoyment.

There's no greater optimist than a reader, always hoping that, despite all the disappointments before it, the next book will bring them the enjoyment that first neck-shivering, heart-fluttering one did. The same, I suppose, could be said of any dreamer.

One of the consolations of age is also one of its desolations: how can we ever feel, much less survive, the passions we once had the energy for when we were younger? What friends do we ever make in adulthood that compare to the ones we made as children? What books can we ever love the way we did the ones when we were young?

But the books I've loved most are those which went beyond mere achievement or entertainment, which I had to keep reading as though my life depended on it, losing all track or sense of time, the uncertain light flickering against the sheets as I read deep into the night and the characters' souls, as though the outside world was a distraction not half as real as the one that bled into my dreams, and which, like me, was utterly changed when I finally looked up to see the faint morning light pry the curtains open, in the way my eyes had been by what I'd read.

The first book I read through the night was *To Kill a Mockingbird*. Like the other night books I'd soon read – *The Catcher in the Rye* or *Lord of the Flies* – the title seemed such a mystery. Everything I'd read before then had the subject in the title, like *The Secret Garden*, *The Magic Pudding*, *Treasure Island*. But how *did* you catch anything in bread? Who *was* the Lord of the Flies? And why would anyone want to kill a mockingbird? Their mysteries seemed secrets, especially as nobody in my family had ever read them, nor were particularly interested in discussing 'something as useless as make-believe', as my father once said.

Yet although a great book speaks for no one, it speaks to everyone. Or as Solnit puts it much more eloquently, 'Writing is saying to the no one who may eventually be the reader those things one has no someone to whom to say them.' Perhaps that's why we consider the books we love, the books that really touched us, to be as dear and cherished as friends, because they say, in ways we can't, things we wished we could. They're not sermons, but conversations, reminding us we're not alone, we're not the only person to feel this way.

When I was a child, they expressed my most cherished hopes and wildest fantasies, saying the things I couldn't say because I didn't have the words or courage to say them. As I grew older, they shared their most secret shames and deepest fears, allowing me to admit – albeit silently – my own. The books that have meant the most to me have felt like the deepest secrets, as though I was the only person to have ever discovered them. But is there any greater elation than discovering someone loves the very same book you thought no one else had heard of? All of a sudden, you share a secret, a dream, a memory, in a way your individual experiences and lives never could.

Sometimes, catching my children up way past their bedtimes, pretending not to read books I once loved at their age in the torch-lit dark, I'll pretend to admonish them, and they'll pretend to put the book away, and I'll be secretly glad that we share a secret, a dream, a memory we could only find together in a book read years apart.

Although I can't remember how I met most people I know – apart from my wife – I can tell you where I bought most of the books on my shelves, even if I can't remember anything about them. I once passed a second-hand bookshop in a desultory lunch hour and went in, not looking for anything but a way to stave off returning to a job I hated. I walked out with two books that changed my life: Somerset Maugham's *The Moon and Sixpence* and Graham Greene's *Travels with My Aunt*. I don't know why I picked them up. Within a month of reading them – one about a retired bank manager who escapes the predictable safety of his suburban retirement and the other about a stockbroker who forsakes everything to become an artist – I'd quit that job I hated and taken a year off to write the novel I'd previously abandoned.

In that year I spent more time procrastinating than writing, but I read voraciously, especially Greene and Maugham. For the first time, I read to understand. Not just to work out how great writers wrote, but how I could make sense of my life, and myself. They didn't tell me what to do or offer me any answers: rather, they asked me to ask the questions of myself I'd tried not to ask. *Could I be a writer? Who was I anyway?*

Reading them, I imagined that if my life flashed before my eyes as I died, what did I want to see? That I'd lived my dreams, or I was being put to sleep by boredom, living the safe, conventional life my parents expected of me?

Like books, of which we can only remember a quote, or a moment, or a name, life's full of those strange, portentous, random moments, in which entire lives – those forgotten and those yet to be conceived – turn on sudden decisions and unsaid words, where the difference between hope and regret are only revealed in the telling, and as difficult to tell apart from memory and imagination, much less the truth.

~

So, if you can recall the question: if we forget most of what we read, then why *do* we read? You might as well ask why we dream, or live at all, given how much we forget of our dreams and lives. Yet just as I cannot imagine being alive without dreams, I couldn't dream of living without reading. One reason we forget books is because, unlike other forms of art, they're so difficult to return to. We can listen to an album over and over until the melody is a part of us, or watch and re-watch a film until we can quote it at will. But all they take is an hour or two each time we watch or listen to them again.

A book demands a deeper investment of concentration and time – at the very least a night of sustained attention. Dreams, too, I suppose, and we all know what happens to them in the morning.

There are some books I could never read again – not just ones I didn't love but especially ones I loved and which have been crucial to my life and work. Who was it who said if you don't love Emma Bovary at twenty, you don't have a heart, and if you still love her at forty, you don't have a head? Our private canons are constantly shifting. Perhaps like life itself, which we can never relive, we can only return to the *memory* of that moment we read the book. Like old love letters or diaries, books we once loved are souvenirs of times we do and don't want to forget, which might be why they're almost impossible to throw away without some sense of loss, even as we cannot recall all the particulars. There's a reason we give new lovers and friends and our children copies of the books we love: we're giving them a part of ourselves in an act of faith even greater than lending them.

Now with so many books to read, I rarely re-read books, especially ones I've loved. I'm too afraid of spoiling my memories of them, such as they are. The irony is that while all writing – whether historical or fictional, a memoir or a shopping list – is driven by an impulse to remember, the simple act of reading is predicated by forgetting. Unhappiness is infinitesimally careful, obsessively going over the same thing, but happiness is infinitely careless, gone before we know it. It's often struck me, woken at 3 am by another nightmare or unbidden regret, how easily we forget what we most want to remember, and how much more easily we remember what we most want to forget. The happiest times fly past as if they never happened; the unhappiest return again and again – is it any coincidence we read so many books we love on holiday?

All that remains of the books I've loved are impressions, just like all the nightmares I've tried to forget. A glass cathedral on a river, a boy made up like a girl in a brothel, a mole in a burrow . . . everything a snatch of something as faint as dreams or childhood memories, and even more evocatively powerful precisely because I can't quite grasp them.

As Salman Rushdie notes, when 'the writer . . . tries to reflect the world, he is obliged to deal in broken mirrors, some of whose fragments have been irretrievably lost. But the broken mirror may actually be as valuable as the one which is supposedly unflawed. The shards of memory acquire greater status, greater resonance because they are *remains*.'

Even though I can't remember all of them, the books I love are still a part of me: reading other books will remind me of them; I'll find myself quoting them in conversation or in my writing – faint memories of names and moments, all swirling, like half-remembered dreams and snatches of childhood memory, to ferment, unseen, in the deep delvèd earth of my subconscious to hopefully pop, sparkling, into my work in ways I can't yet imagine.

The more I read, the more I write, and the more I write, the more I read: each informs the other, and when creative writing students say they don't read because they don't want their work to be influenced by others, I have to ask – having endured more creative writing workshops than I care to remember – surely that can't be a *bad* thing?

Reading and writing, involving the same focused concentration, are as close as I get to meditation. The one thing I remember from Alain de Botton's *The Romantic Movement* was the observation that some people read for escapism, others for self-discovery. But for me, there's an element of both. Given how distracted I am when I'm not writing, and how much of my life I've forgotten, it seems strange to say that when I'm really reading, really writing, I feel more alive than when I'm not.

David Foster Wallace said that all the distractions of the modern world that chased away loneliness made him forget his name. But when I read, I don't merely forget the trials of my own life – my petty neuroses and pointless worries, the reverberating whorl of self-commentary and thought and chatter that fills my head day and night, the noise of it competing with the car alarms and advertisements and voices on the TV or radio or internet – more importantly, I forget myself. Reading and writing are a reprieve for me from myself, helping me transcend myself, to become part of something I can barely imagine, and in that reprieve, when I truly lose myself, they also offer me a chance to find myself in the lives and hearts of the people about whom I'm reading or writing, that connection and compassion that puts me in someone else's skin and soul, and sees the world with new eyes: theirs.

Some might say such 'imaginative empathy' is an illusion. But perhaps everything and everyone is, depending on what eye beholds them, what they happen to remember and choose to forget, what stories they tell us, and themselves.

Fiction is the most fundamental human art, according to Jonathan Franzen. 'Fiction is storytelling, and our reality arguably consists of the stories we tell about ourselves,' Franzen says. More than this, or what we remember, it's made up of what we believe. Belief is an extension of that humane imagination. We want more than anything to believe, and we readily suspend our disbelief in religion, in love, in fiction: what part of the bible said that 'belief is the reality of things hoped for, the evidence of things unseen'? Belief helps us to see the meaning in the contradictions and confusions, the randomness and meaninglessness of the world and in ourselves. And it's in suspending our disbelief as we read that we can come closer to feeling that understanding: of the world, of ourselves and of each other.

This is the almost religious, meditative transcendence of the simple act of reading: that in losing ourselves in the lives of others, we can find ourselves, enabling us to see the world and those around us refracted in a new light – in our own reflection.

Where else in the world can we do that? Not even in our dreams.

'Language is for invention and creativity and the craic.
And collaborative reading is just that: a lot of craic.'

GABRIELLE CAREY

The Not So Simple Act of (Collaborative) Reading

Gabrielle Carey

In memory of Gerry Taheny

EVEN THIRTY YEARS AFTER THE PUBLICATION OF *Puberty Blues*, it's a question that I am still regularly asked. Mostly out of curiosity but occasionally out of suspicion. 'How did you write a book *together*?'

I talk about composing each sentence collaboratively, sharing ideas about what would come next and how it would be phrased, as well as editing as we wrote. It's a difficult concept for people to grasp because writing is usually a solitary act, possibly even an intimate one – just like reading. Intimate because the reader, often in bed at night, engages with the author precisely in order to be aroused – by feelings of excitement, stimulation, sadness, terror and wonder. So what happens when this intimate act, involving one person, becomes a group act, involving several? Is it like progressing from quiet coupling to group sex?

When James Joyce was asked how anyone could be expected to understand his final work, he answered, 'It is all so simple; if anyone doesn't understand a passage, all he need do is read it aloud.' But reading aloud is preferable when you have someone to read aloud to. And that's where collaborative reading comes in.

For the past ten years I have been reading *Finnegans Wake* aloud with a small group around my kitchen table. It has been a scintillating, frustrating, enlightening experience, but most of all it has been funny. And filthy. If the censors thought *Ulysses* was obscene, they would have thought *Finnegans Wake* positively pornographic. That is, if they'd bothered to read it.

Since its publication in 1939, *Finnegans Wake* has remained largely unread, except by a handful of eccentrics and academics. But change is stirring. According to an online directory, there are now a total of thirty-three groups meeting regularly to read *Finnegans Wake* aloud, in London, York, Glasgow, Dublin, Belfast, New York, Zurich, Adelaide, Brisbane and Sydney. A critically acclaimed theatre adaptation of *Finnegans Wake* had a sell-out season in London, and at the Sydney Theatre in 2015. And a recent 2014 lecture at the Royal Institute of Philosophy in London described the *Wake* as 'a masterwork for contemporary globalising cultures'.

Masterwork? I hear you say. But isn't it all a load of gobbledygook written in an unintelligible, made-up language? Or, as H. G. Wells accused, 'A tangled prose almost indistinguishable from the gibberings of a lunatic.'

It's true that the language of the *Wake* is not your ordinary, everyday English. Joyce called it night-time language. *Ulysses* was a book of the day, he said, and *Finnegans Wake* the book of the night. So the book makes sense in the same way that dreams do and don't. But that's the whole idea – to challenge our usual way of 'making sense'; Joyce asks us instead to 'pleasekindly communicake with the original sinse'.

I've never read Joyce and I never intend to, I hear you say next. But if you think you haven't read Joyce, think again.

'Even those who read very few novels encounter the effects of Joyce's revolution every week, if not every day,' says scholar Derek

Attridge, 'in television and video, film, popular music, and advertising, all of which are marked as modern genres by the use of Joycean techniques of parody and pastiche, self-referentiality, fragmentation of word and image, open-ended narrative, and multiple point of view.'

But what is *Finnegans Wake* about? I now hear you ask, somewhat tentatively.

Everything. It's a history of the world, the story of Adam and Eve, of sin and redemption, of rise and fall, of Humpty Dumpty falling off the wall and Irish Tim Finnegan, from the folk ballad of the book's title, falling off his ladder (drunk, of course). It's simultaneously encyclopaedic and anti-encyclopaedia. Like an *Encyclopaedia Britannica* mash-up. Among other things, Joyce described it as, 'a meanderthalltale', 'a Wholesale Safety Pun factory', 'a wonderful game', and a 'collideorscape'.

Over the years membership of the *Finnegans Wake* reading group has fluctuated: some have stayed for half an hour, others for half a decade. Because the *Wake* is cyclic, rather than linear, you can enter the text at any point, like a river. In fact, rivers run throughout the *Wake* in a way that makes them much more than a recurring motif; over six hundred of the world's rivers are mentioned, with particular attention to Dublin's River Liffey, and indeed, the very first word of this extraordinary work is 'riverrun'.

'riverrun' is in lower-case because the book begins and ends mid-sentence, the last word leading back to the beginning. Finnegan is also a play on words – Finn: end, egan: again – as well as a reference to the ditty *Michael Finnegan*, which, incidentally, I learnt in the playground of Sutherland North Primary School in 1966. We all held hands in a circle and sang:

There was an old man called Michael Finnegan
He grew whiskers on his chin again
The wind came up and blew them in again
Poor old Michael Finnegan. *Begin again!*

And then we would go back to the beginning of the song, repeating the absurdist story of whiskers growing inward and outward at the behest of the breeze. (It was from this moment that I developed my fondness for musical rounds, canons and all forms of contrapuntal music, which later manifested as *The Contrapunks*, a recorder ensemble that premiered in the Caringbah High School auditorium in 1977.)

Perhaps it was this musical foundation that helped me get my first taste for *Finnegans Wake*, a book that was written as much for the ear as the eye, partly because Joyce was going blind as he wrote it. The many voices and meanings interweaving simultaneously makes it comparable to a fugue and means the best way to engage with the book is to listen first, for the sound and the music, and consider the meaning second.

So how does collaborative reading actually work? This is where the simple act of reading begins. We take turns, usually just a few paragraphs at a time, and then we discuss. Let me give you an example. Here's one sentence describing a kiss:

> For it was then a pretty thing happened of pure diversion mayhap, when his flattering hend, at the justright moment, like perchance some cook of corage might clip the lad on a poot of porage, handshut his duckhouse, the vivid girl, deaf with love (ah sure, you know her, our angel being, one of romance's fadeless wonderwomen, and, sure now, we all know you dote on her even unto date!), with a queeleetlecree of joysis crisis she renulited their disunited, with ripy lepes to ropy lopes (the dear o'dears!) and the golden importunity of aloofer's leavetime, when, as quick as greased pigskin, Amoricas Champias, with one aragan throast, druve the massive of virilrightjinghangshot into the goal of her gullet.

The couple are Tristan and Isolde, from the legendary story of adultery between an Irish princess and a Cornish knight. Isolde, overcome with desire and in the traditional bold manner of Celtic maidens, initiates the kiss by reuniting her 'ripy lepes' (ruby lips) while letting out a 'queeleetlecree' (queer little cry) of 'joysis crisis' (joy, Jesus Christ). Tristan seizes this 'golden importunity of aloofer's leavetime' (a lover's lifetime) as quick as 'greased pigskin' (American slang for football) and with one arrogant thrust, drives his 'massive' (missive, message, tongue) into Isolde's gullet.

So, after half an hour, that's what our group made of one sentence from *Finnegans Wake*. If we keep going at this rate we'll finish the book in 2029.

Of course, the comments above are not exhaustive or comprehensive; it's simply an attempt to unravel the infinitely unravelable. The purpose is to have fun, and another reason for the title – taken from an Irish ballad's refrain: 'Lots of fun at Finnegan's wake.' When you see something in a word or words that you haven't seen before, it's like looking at one of those visual puzzles and suddenly seeing the pattern. It feels exciting and satisfying and fosters a dynamic rather than a passive approach to reading. We don't expect to 'get' all the meanings available in *Finnegans Wake*. No one has, or probably ever will.

Joyce promised that *Finnegans Wake* would keep the academics wondering, puzzling and theorising for decades to come. And, as usual, he was right. There are large chunks of the *Wake* that are still a mystery to even the most dedicated Joycean scholars. Nevertheless, amid all the obscurity, even the most amateur of readers can find comedy and obscenity, as well as profound ideas about history, time, literature, language, music, men, women, memory and meaning-making. It is not true that *Finnegans Wake* doesn't make sense; it's just a different kind of sense than the one we are used to. To uncover this different sense one has to develop not only a different way of reading, but also a different way of thinking and a different idea about the purpose of language.

The Wakean way of thinking derives partly from the influence of the Irish language on the English. One of the main differences between English and Irish, according to writer John Banville, is that the Irish language has a kind of in-built ambiguity. 'On the other hand,' says Banville, 'English is a language of command, a declarative language, which constantly seeks to be rid of ambiguity. English writers constantly seek for clarity and avoid ambiguity. They follow Orwell's dictum that prose should be a plain sheet of glass through which you look; but for us Irish writers writing in English, language is a lens and we know that it distorts and we glory in the fact that it distorts, and we also want people to admire how beautifully polished the lens is . . . so there is an essential difference . . . between an Irish writer writing in English and an English writer.

'Irish is a very oblique language. It's very hard to say direct things in Irish. You can't say, "I'm a man." You have to say, "I'm in my manness." Sometimes I think it's more a mode of evasion rather than communication.'

The obvious explanation for a habit of evasive speech is centuries of oppressive colonisation. But maybe that's not the entire answer. Maybe the Irish, as reflected in their language, have an entirely different idea about what language is for. Perhaps the Anglo culture believes language is essentially for communicating clear messages containing useful information whereas the Irish believe language is about storytelling and socialising. The content, therefore, is not primary. It's about how it's told, where and with whom. Or, as Anglo-Irish literary theorist Terry Eagleton says, 'Language is first of all a way of being with other people, and only secondarily about getting things done. This is why the paradigm of human communication is not the public relations agency but the pub.' No coincidence then that the 'main character' of *Finnegans Wake* is a publican. Language, and therefore reading, is not intended to be a clear morse code whose primary function is the efficient transmission of information. Language is for invention and creativity and the *craic*. And collaborative reading is just that: a lot of *craic*.

After a decade of monthly meetings, our group has reached page 399. Only 229 pages to go. Our running joke is that we'll be dead before we finish. At least it was a running joke until Gerry, our cherished fellow Finnster from Sligo, announced his diagnosis of pancreatic cancer. And we were only up to page 287.

I had known for a good while that *Finnegans Wake* was an antidepressant and that collaborative reading of the *Wake* can bring immediate and tangible health benefits – not least because of the belly laughs – but until Gerry's illness I'd never thought of the *Wake* as essential to palliative care. I won't claim that *Finnegans Wake* can save lives, but I will claim that it is a kind of magic pudding that you can share and enjoy, right to the last. It is a world without end, or as Joyce puts it, 'whorled without aimed'.

One of the very last *Wake* groups that Gerry attended was on the twenty-ninth floor of the Zenith building in Kings Cross, where one of our members had recently bought an apartment. The views from all three balconies were stunning but we weren't looking. Our eyes, as usual, were focused on the page. Gerry had arrived with his medication and was careful to drink only weak tea. For the first time we noticed that he was, unsurprisingly, deeply depressed. Until we came to the following passage:

> Are you right there Michael, are you right? Do you think you can hold on by sitting tight? Well, of course, it's awful angelous. Still I don't feel it's so dangelous. Ay, I'm right here, Nickel, and I'll write. Singing the top line why it suits me mikey fine. But, yaghags hogwarts and arrahquinouthiance, it's the muddest thick that was ever heard dump since Eggasmather got smothered in the plap of the pfan.

On one level, this is just another lavatory joke. Joyce is famously known for his scatalogical obsession. Michael, the first archangel, who often represents God, is 'sitting tight' on the toilet. It is typical of Joyce to have a deity taking a dump – he enjoys combining the sacred and the dirty, and doesn't shy away from shit in any form, even 'the muddest thick that was ever heard dump' in a toilet 'pfan' (which is also 'the maddest thing'). But the phrase, 'Are you right there Michael, are you right?' also refers to a famous Irish song about the notoriously unreliable nineteenth-century train between Clare and Ennis in Ireland. So Gerry, the group's authority on Irish folklore and traditional music, immediately burst into song:

> Are ye right there, Michael, are ye right?
> Do you think that ye'll be home before it's light?
> 'Tis all dependin' whether the ould engin' howlds together
> Still it might now, Michael
> So it might!

Like so many stories in the *Wake*, the song is based on a real incident. In 1897 a train carrying a well-known Irish performer from Ennis to Kilkee broke down. The songster, Percy French, was late for his concert and filed a suit against the railroad for 'loss of profits', which he won. When he later composed a song about his experience, it was so popular that the railway considered suing for libel. So, as we have come to expect while reading this extraordinary work, we learn a snippet of history – about railroads in Ireland, about musical traditions and about a minor historical figure. And we also find 'hogwarts' which, until the Harry Potter phenomenon, was just another weird word in the *Wake* and now is famously associated with wizardry.

But the real magic for our group was the sight of Gerry, suddenly transforming from a despondent cancer-sufferer into a sparked-up entertainer. By the end of our reading he was visibly re-energised.

A couple of months later, I visited Gerry in Concord Centre for Palliative Care. He had only two books by his bed, both studies of Joyce. Our very last discussion was about Joyce's famous inversion of the concept of the epiphany. (Epiphany was originally a religious term, but Joyce reclaimed the word for the ordinary person, believing that we were all capable of sudden insights of transforming and transcendental meaning.)

In his last few days, Gerry was still chasing meaning, still enjoying 'the wonderful game' offered by the playfulness of Joyce's final text. Perhaps he would have accepted death with grace and dignity without the help of the *Wake*, but I'm certain it helped. And the fact that the book's title was inspired by a post-mortem party – 'Lots of fun at Finnegan's wake!' – is also a reminder that parties and funerals, fun and tragedy, life and death, are inseparable oppositions. And that all oppositions are complementary, as Joyce contends, and will therefore find final rest in reunion.

Gerry died on 17 July 2014. Although quietly atheist, his last words to me, and to all his friends, were, 'God bless.'

Finnegans Wake is similarly contradictory. Shockingly blasphemous, it is also full of prayers:

> O Loud, here the wee beseech of thees, of each of these thy unlitten ones! Grant sleep in hour's time, O Loud! . . .
>
> Loud, heap miseries upon us yet entwine our arts with laughters low!

So that is the story of the book I have been reading for more than a decade and the joy that the not so simple act of reading James Joyce has brought to me as an individual reader but also as a collaborative reader. Our group continues, with one empty chair honouring our missing colleague. Reading the *Wake* reminds us of Gerry's irreplaceableness because no one knows Irish folk songs the way he did and none of us speak fluent Irish as Gerry did. Now that he has gone, there are also references and meanings in the text that will no longer be available to us. There will be a meaningful absence always. But the *Wake* will continue, forever celebrating life, death and language.

'The Plains *became for me an iconic book, a black diamond, a Rosetta Stone.'*

WAYNE MACAULEY

Far Enough: The Peculiar World of *The Plains*

Wayne Macauley

THE DUSTJACKET OF THE FIRST EDITION OF *THE PLAINS* describes it as 'a lament for an Australian literature that has never been written'. Thirty years later, this strange, disquieting, curious little book continues to stand almost alone in the library of alternative Australian fiction. But make no mistake: this is no archaeological artefact. *The Plains* is a masterpiece, and, word for word, sentence for sentence, one of the best novels ever written in this country.

Like all great allegories, its premise is simple. A filmmaker, researching a script to be called *The Interior*, journeys to the flat plains of the inland where in a remote town he spends his days in the pub trying to learn what he can about the so-called plainsmen and their peculiar way of life. Because it *is* peculiar. Like the many other petitioners who have made the journey ('I cannot even say that at a certain hour I knew I had left Australia') in the hope of finding a patron among the wealthy landowners there, our narrator must work hard to understand their culture – detailed, arcane and to the outsider utterly foreign – if he is to find favour with them.

It is right that a peculiar literary work should have a peculiar publishing history. Murnane had originally written a work of about 60,000 words, *The Only Adam*, with the opening and closing sections set in a place 'that might have stood in relation to the setting of the rest of the book as a mirage stands in relationship to the landscape that gives rise to it'. Bruce Gillespie, the publisher at Norstrilia, a small press specialising in sci-fi and speculative fiction (Murnane: 'I would have thought that *all* fiction is speculative'), suggested that if *The Only Adam* failed to find a publisher he would like to include 'the plains sections' in an anthology he was planning. The longer work never did find a home, and Murnane decided to explore his mirage further. 'It seemed to me,' he told me recently, 'that I could write more than I had already written about my mysterious plains.' In 1982 Gillespie published this 30,000-word manuscript in a handsome hardback.

When I first read *The Plains*, in my late twenties, I noted in my diary that it was 'miles beyond most other Australian writing I've read'. I had already given White a fair go, and Stead; I had read most of Lawson and stumbled my way through that other great curio, Joseph Furphy's *Such Is Life*. I'd read some early Carey and Bail, and was keeping up where I could with the little magazines and journals. But *The Plains* was something else. Here was a stepping-off into an alternative world as exhilarating as anything proposed by Swift, Kafka, Borges or Calvino, written in prose to rival the European greats I had already fallen in love with. And, more importantly, in the subtle cultural investigations going on deep within the book, Murnane seemed to be forging his own way not just towards an alternative Australian literature but an alternative way of imagining the country. With an eye both to the European and South American avant-garde, combined with hefty doses of Proust and Kerouac – most evident in his extraordinary debut novel, *Tamarisk Row* – he was out on his own making something eccentric, free-floating and completely new.

Because let's not forget, aside from its startling originality, *The Plains* is also a very funny book. In the early pages especially, Murnane maps our national anxieties – the paranoia about who we are and what we might be, the idea that culture is always somehow elsewhere – with a withering sense of humour. Where explorers like Thomas Livingstone Mitchell (quoted in the epigraph) saw this continent's inland as a blank slate, *The Plains* dares us to see it otherwise. Yes, the interior, that vast, empty space we coast-dwellers habitually turn our backs on, is forbidding, but it is by no means bereft. While we've been gazing across the ocean, something peculiar has been going on behind our backs. The imaginative leap of *The Plains* is to reverse the comfortable order of the idea of culture being 'over there' and to see instead Australia's interior as a richly storied other world. The people who dwell out on the plains are not cringing hicks. They're experimentalists. They're cutting edge. They're everything we coast-dwellers are not.

In the dialogues of the landowners, in the narrator's musings in the pub and then as he wanders the vast library of his patron, in the way he watches his patron's daughter and wife ('still beautiful according to the conventions of the plains') moving among the estate's gardens and lawns, we see a world shimmering with speculation and wonder. The plains' history is so rich and its arts and sciences so sophisticated that they challenge anything old Europe has to offer, and the plainsmen themselves – deep-thinking, serious and culturally alert – 'confront even the most obdurate or the most ingenuous work utterly receptive and willing'. No, this is not the inland of lonely truck stops and whistling wires and fat guys fishing the last potato cake out of the bain-marie. Out on Murnane's plains you get everything: the great perplexity of human existence, the itch of human flesh, the tug on the heart, the dreamy imagining of togetherness, the comedy of trying. Here is the narrator planning his courtship of his patron's wife:

As soon as I had finished my preliminary notes for *The Interior*, and before I began work on the filmscript itself, I would write a short work – probably a collection of essays – which would settle things between the woman and myself. I would have it published privately under one of the seldom-used imprints that my patron reserves for his clients' work-in-progress or marginalia. And I would so arrange the ostensible subject-matter of the work that the librarians here would insert a copy among the shelves where she spends her afternoons.

I foresaw this much of my scheme happening as I had planned it. The only uncertain item was the last – I had no way of ensuring that the woman would open my book during her lifetime . . .

Dear Gerald,
This is a letter I have been meaning to write for a very long time. I first read *The Plains* in 1985 and it had a profound effect on me. At the time I was a 27-year-old writer wondering if there was any new Australian literature I was ever going to like, let alone get inspiration from. Your book gave me great faith in continuing to pursue the writing I had been doing – writing, it's true, that never looked like getting published but was nonetheless, I think, true to itself and its creator . . .

This is the first paragraph of a letter I wrote to Gerald Murnane in 2002. I was at the time a forty-four-year-old writer about to have his first book published. We are, all of us, at some point, I think, looking for some line of steerage, something to set our course by, some little marker buoy out there somewhere that tells us we're not completely lost. This is what *The Plains* was for me. This little book, written in my city by a person twenty years my senior, living in a suburb just a stone's throw away, somehow made everything right. By that time

I'd read and loved Hamsun, Walser, Kafka, Gombrowicz, Beckett and others, but there was no one in Australia who spoke to me in the same way. *The Plains* became for me an iconic book, a black diamond, a Rosetta Stone.

It was about the feat of imagination – how many Australian books dared go where this one went? – but it was also about the marks on the paper. Few living writers anywhere are as ambitious with the prose form as Gerald Murnane. He fills his works with sentences so boldly constructed and so beautifully finished that any writer serious about their craft would be well advised to spend some time with them: the subtle unreeling of the narrative, the phrases creeping one by one towards a distantly observed idea, the hand-on-mouth humour, the firm and steady gaze. You might not know where Murnane is taking you, but you can't help being taken.

> The countless volumes of this library are close-set with so much speculative prose, so many chapters after chapters appear in parentheses, such glosses and footnotes surround the thin trickles of actual text that I fear to discover in some unexceptional essay by a plainsman of no great reputation a tentative paragraph describing a man not unlike myself speculating endlessly about the plains but never setting foot in them . . .

Gerald and I have continued to exchange letters over the years. Some time ago, in place of a letter, he sent me a photo of a straight road cutting a line through the Wimmera Plains towards Mount Arapiles in the distance. His note to me was written on the back. He was, he said, 'in excellent health and spirits', had a new work on the go and would soon have his tenth book published. I looked at that photo for a long time: the straight road, the low horizon, the big blue sky. Gerald Murnane, author of *The Plains*, was writing to me from them.

We met for the first time in 2012, at an event to celebrate the book's reissue as part of the Text Classics series. Text was now my publisher, and had invited me to write the introduction. (It seemed a long way back to that young man's diary entry, the middle-aged man's fawning letter.) I'd presumed Gerald and I were going to be interviewed together, as a double act, but when I got there I was told I would be interviewing *him*. After my first stumbling question we got into our stride and it ended up a great night for all. Later, on the way out (I nearly forgot), I pulled out my old Norstrilia edition, its dust jacket still intact, and asked if he would sign it for me. He looked a little surprised, me carrying around this ancient artefact. When I slipped the signed copy back into its place on my shelf later that evening, I felt like a long chapter had closed.

So what is this thing we might call an alternative Australian literature and what would it look like? The last word might come from one of the earliest passages in *The Plains*. Compelled one day in the pub to tell the plainsmen his own story before they will let him listen to theirs, the narrator says, 'I told them a story almost devoid of events or achievements. Outsiders would have made little of it, but the plainsmen understood.'

If you believe yourself a plainsman or woman, I urge you to seek out, read, laugh at, enjoy and be inspired by this extraordinary book.

'I remember how those few lines of verse captured my own imagination . . . and bound me to something that is not too fanciful to call destiny.'

DEBRA ADELAIDE

The Tower

Debra Adelaide

BUILDING 1, THE INFAMOUS UTS TOWER. THIS MIGHT seem an unlikely place to inspire images of legendary Arthurian characters, early Victorian poetry, the nineteenth-century artist John William Waterhouse's painting of a woman in a boat, and the movie version of *The Prime of Miss Jean Brodie*, but these are all in my head at once.

I am lecturing on Jessica Anderson's novel *Tirra Lirra by the River*. First, I quote some poetry.

On either side the river lie
Long fields of barley and of rye,
That clothe the wold and meet the sky;
And through the field the road runs by
  To many-towered Camelot;
And up and down the people go,
Gazing where the lilies blow
Round an island there below,
  The island of Shalott.

Willows whiten, aspens quiver,
Little breezes dusk and shiver
Through the wave that runs for ever
By the island in the river
    Flowing down to Camelot.
Four gray walls, and four gray towers,
Overlook a space of flowers,
And the silent isle imbowers
    The Lady of Shalott.

A portion of Tennyson's *The Lady of Shalott* appears early in Anderson's novel, on page nine of the Penguin edition, the section introducing Sir Lancelot and his song, which explains the rather odd title of the novel. What could this nineteenth-century ballad and a slender, late twentieth-century Australian novel have in common? Alfred, Lord Tennyson, was poet laureate, wrote Queen Victoria's favourite poem, *In Memorium*, and was the epitome of the Victorian public artistic figure. Tennyson, it has been said, not only embodied the age of Tennyson, but also outlived it.

The story of *The Lady of Shalott* is partly derived from myths of Sir Lancelot, emblematic knight errant, archetypal seductive male and rival to King Arthur himself. Embodying the golden dream of Camelot, he also destroys it, leading to civil war and darkening political times for England. Lancelot is chivalry gone sour.

Tennyson's Lady is a magical being, condemned to live in a tower by a river and weave her tapestries. Forbidden to look out at the world directly, she may only experience it via reflection in her large crystal mirror. But, tormented by desire, and by longing to escape, seduced by the song of Lancelot outside, the Lady resists her fate and gazes directly out of the window at the world. Leaving her tower, she takes a boat down the river towards Camelot, lies back in it and dies. The moment is captured in John William Waterhouse's famous 1888 painting.

Once I knew the entire poem by heart, but that does not concern me now. The question now is not what this poem is all about, nor even how it relates to *Tirra Lirra by the River*, but why, when I quote this verse, I hear a girl's voice, an English voice, with clear vowel sounds, and why I see a group of schoolgirls and their teacher, with burnished red-gold hair, her hand placed expressively at her throat.

> She left the web, she left the loom,
> She made three paces through the room,
> She saw the water-lily bloom,
> She saw the helmet and the plume,
>   She looked down to Camelot.

These lines are quoted by Sandy, the favourite of Jean Brodie's students in *The Prime of Miss Jean Brodie*. I cannot now remember if I read the book first or saw the movie. The novel was published in 1961 and the movie appeared in 1969 when I was eleven. I know I was in my late teens when I first encountered either, or both. And I remember how those few lines of verse captured my own imagination – just as Lancelot's song captures that of the Lady – and bound me to something that is not too fanciful to call destiny. Muriel Spark led me to Tennyson, and Tennyson allowed me to start reading for myself, which led me to the remainder of my life.

The honours year in the English department of Sydney University in 1980 was said to be rigorous. I found it hard work but thrilling. I was a glutton for reading, desperate for an education in literature, even more desperate for guidance in reading, something I had never had: instructed to buy myself a few books in my final year of school, I had roamed the shelves of the local bookshop, with barely an idea of what to choose. By studying literature I was determined to understand that mysterious quality known as 'culture', which I expected would be found in books. Culture was always unreachable, somewhere else. It was almost regarded with suspicion. 'Oh, they're *cultured* people,' was a phrase from my suburban childhood, meaning people who read certain books, went to the opera and ballet and followed other forms of art. Cultured people watched the ABC and subscribed to the theatre. People like us took in the *Daily Mirror* and went to movie nights at the St George Leagues Club.

For the honours thesis, or long essay, we were encouraged to write about whatever topic we wanted. Honours student refugees from another university, who had left their English department en masse to enrol in ours, told horror stories of how their professor had *told* them what they would be doing for their theses. But here in the Woolley Building, there was no pressure to be a Marxist, a structuralist or a postcolonialist, to study world or local literatures, to prioritise popular or classic literature. We were as free as the breeze to float around in arcane Victoriana, to dive into the vast sea of criticism on Keats' odes, to revisit Elizabethan love poetry or Shakespeare's comedies, or to investigate the minor Brontë oeuvre, Melville's *Moby-Dick* or Richardson's *The Fortunes of Richard Mahony*. Such were the diverse interests of the huge academic staff, you could have proposed a thesis on the chapter epigraphs of *Middlemarch*, on piscatorial poetry, or on the blank pages of *Tristram Shandy* and found someone qualified to supervise you. It was a place for eccentric and shameless specialisation. Which is how I was allowed to concentrate on Tennyson's unpublished yet not unproductive years 1833–1842.

I did not know then that I was a consummate romantic. Only now, decades later, do I understand my attraction to *The Lady of Shalott*, and to Jean Brodie, and my subsequent obsession with not only this poem but many others of Tennyson. He was a Victorian poet with a romantic core, and appealed to many of us at the time, all searching for escape. Tennyson's Lady, Miss Jean Brodie, are the archetypal dreamers and romantics, defined by yearning. Miss Brodie is one of literature's most brilliant and enduring characters because she is more than her author's creation – she has created a narrative of her own life, with romantic touches (a lover killed in the Great War), glamour and status (her audience with the Pope), with embellishments, secrets and lies, with sexual adventures and of course even her own language. My prime, my prime, my prime: this echoes through the novel like a mantra, the chorus of her performances. Miss Brodie does not live, she performs. Lover of story, of the holiday anecdote or the wartime melodrama, she invents narrative wherever she goes. Tennyson's Lady is cursed not to engage directly in life, and can only glimpse the world outside her tower obliquely through her mirror. Despite her energy and anti-parochialism, her European holidays and excursions to museums and galleries, Miss Brodie actually views life more than she experiences it, and when she does experience it, it is vicariously, her mirror being the girls she is teaching.

Light years from Arthurian or Victorian England, from Edinburgh of the 1930s or even the 1960s, when Spark's novel enjoyed its first success, I was nevertheless the Lady. Or at least in my imagination, were I beautiful, talented and possessed of exquisite sensibility. I was yearning to escape, though in my case the tower was formed of elements such as a limited imagination, a suburban existence, a repression of soul and art and sex so profound I wonder it did not at times appear branded on my forehead. 'Education means a leading out,' intones Miss Brodie, in her compressed philosophy of education, 'e, out and duco, I lead.' I draw out. I do not put in, I do not impose.

Naturally, this is one of the greatest lies in a novel stuffed with them, but nevertheless my romantic soul responded to this too. To have teachers like Miss Brodie, who suspended normal lessons for sessions on art and current affairs, who took students outdoors to sit on the lawn and recite poetry and eat special treats. Who recounted dramatic tales of personal or national history, postures erect, heads thrown back, eyes half-closed. Who stood at the window and directed our gaze to a world beyond our limited horizons . . .

How I would have loved to have even heard of *The Lady of Shalott* at the age of twelve. I could have been Muriel Spark's Sandy reciting those stanzas as the girls sit on the lawn of the Marcia Blaine schoolyard. If I ever became a teacher (I never seriously considered it, though I entertained fantasies of possessing such allure and power) I would bring passion and commitment to the job. I would be a graceful, elegant, witty, confident pedagogue, effortlessly drawing younger, ignorant, wondering students along in my wake as I sailed serenely through their education. In short, I would be everything I was not.

This is why I read, of course; it is why I have always read. Within a book, I become another person entirely.

It would be impossible to overstate the popularity of *The Lady of Shalott* to Victorian readers and subsequent generations. It has been a perennial staple of the school recitation, and evidently was to Spark, writing about the pre-war generation of schoolgirls. There is first the simple pull of its song-like lyrics, its repeated refrains, its spell-like cadences. Then there is the tug of its powerful mythologies, and its endless ambiguities. Who is the Lady? Why is she cursed? Why must she die? What is the symbolism of the tower? The mirror? The tapestry? It is no wonder that the critical literature on this poem is vast.

But I was aware of none of this when I first fixated on Tennyson as an undergraduate. Aware only that I wanted to re-read this poem, I devised an honours thesis that would allow me to explore the poem's own rewriting in an essay discussing his 1832 poems and the so-called ten years' silence in which the poet published nothing. To *The Lady of Shalott* and other poems I applied the sort of intense close reading that triumphed in scrutinising individual lines, words and even punctuation. Very soon I would recognise this analytical approach as claustrophobic and limiting. Unfortunately this happened just after I had finished my thesis, when I read William Empson's *Seven Types of*

Ambiguity and recognised what I had done – not that my work displayed any of this critic's prodigious intelligence and grace.

Naturally there are multiple readings of this poem, just as, years later, I suggested to my students, there are multiple readings of Anderson's novel, *Tirra Lirra by the River*. Sexuality and the artistic temperament are linked, as they are in so many texts, and the female figures in these tales are all about denial and repression. Though absent of any sex scene, *The Prime of Miss Jean Brodie* is deeply concerned with sex and sexuality. As a teacher Jean Brodie is destined to remain single and as a woman in pre-war Edinburgh, to deny her sexual desires. And Anderson's protagonist Nora Porteous's one instance of post-divorce sexual life is so disastrous that she rejects a sexual and love life forever. The Lady of Shalott is the archetypal repressed female and repressed artist, the weaver of magic webs, unable to participate directly in the real world. Miss Brodie is similarly this artist: passionate yet repressed, possessed of the capacity to identify and appreciate art, yet not herself create it, and forever seeking to fulfil her destiny through the lives of others, her girls.

At the time of my honours year I was aware that I was being allowed to read and interpret poetry for myself, to follow my nose. The value of this freedom and indulgence only became apparent in later years. And it has taken me a lifetime of reading to understand something simple but vital: children, young adults, anyone, need to follow their reading noses, always. A good thirty-five years after I first heard it, standing in that lecture room in the brown-grey Tower, I remembered above all the irresistible tug of Miss Brodie's voice, and the attraction of the novel, which I first responded to instinctively.

But now that I have thought all this through I realise it is neither Tennyson nor Spark that is at the root of the romantic thread that has run through my life. It is instead a book I read when I was a child, a book I still have, and which introduced me to the world of Arthurian myth and legend, *King Arthur and the Knights of the Round Table.* (I was yet to learn about T. E. White's more famous *Once and Future King.*) This book is a Dean & Son publication, undated, and 'retold' by Phyllis Briggs (a name of pleasing assonance). The Dean's Classics series, according to the back cover, included titles not now regarded as children's books – Charlotte Brontë's *Villette,* Charles Dickens' *A Tale of Two Cities,* John Bunyan's *The Pilgrim's Progress* – but which, back before the invention of children's literature (and perhaps of childhood as we now understand it), were held up as examples of edifying texts. I remember reading many of the Dean's Classics when I was a child, and owning a couple: Anna Sewell's *Black Beauty,* Johanna Spyri's *Heidi.*

Though it is not stated, the inside front cover implies that Phyllis Briggs' retelling of the stories of King Arthur was based on *Le Morte d'Arthur* by Sir Thomas Malory, published in 1485 by William Caxton. Chapter 28 of *King Arthur and the Knights of the Round Table* is 'The Fair Maiden of Astolat' and its story of the Lady of Shalott is more detailed than Tennyson's. Here, Lancelot meets Elaine, the young daughter of a knight, at her father's castle at Astalot, on his way to a tournament at Camelot and she falls in love with him instantly. However, he cannot reciprocate, and as her love deepens Lancelot's unease develops, until he rejects a suggestion that they become a romantic pair. 'Can you not love her in return?' asks his cousin, and Lancelot replies shortly, 'No, I cannot. Love is not to be commanded!' Just before dying of her love, Elaine asks her father to dress her in cloth of gold and place her in a barge to be steered down the Thames to Westminster, where the court resides, so she may pass close to Lancelot one last time.

This is the story I read as a child and while I did study Malory's *Le Morte d'Arthur* later it is this version that remains imprinted in my imagination. This Lady is not an artist or a weaver of tapestries or even possessed of magic properties, but just a girl in love with an ideal.

Tennyson's 1842 revision of the poem is the version that we read today, intriguingly but not substantially changed, and technically tight. So tight that words are missing, in the very first line – 'On either side the river lie' – where a preposition is sacrificed for metre and where the assonance is emphasised so that the line, like the river, simply glides. There are no false notes in *The Lady of Shalott*, and not only are there no extraneous words, there are lexical elisions that reinforce its protagonist's plight. Surely I am not the only reader to wonder at the Lady's first utterance: 'I am half-sick of shadows.'

This, perhaps, is why Jessica Anderson chose this of all poems to capture and reflect (and reflection is vital to both texts) the plight of Nora in *Tirra Lirra by the River.* The compression in this story is astonishing, its complexities endless, and a great deal of its narrative relies directly on what is not said.

Gymea High School, with its industrial blocks, its huge asphalt quadrangle boasting one abject sapling, its grounds of leaf and bark litter and dry sandy soil, was as far from the Marcia Blaine School for Girls as one could imagine. But I had a teacher a little like Miss Brodie once. She was commanding, even imperious, although she possessed a shrill, grating voice, and could be a harsh disciplinarian. But she was also passionate and imaginative, and while she tolerated no nonsense in her English classes, she deplored the physical punishment that was then regularly given to boys. She had stand-up fights with other teachers over this, and one day came to class in angry tears having just witnessed a caning by the English master. The collective attitude was that we loathed this teacher, and students mocked her annoying voice, but privately I admired her. She did not compromise. She had been forced to teach commerce when she was trained in English and history, and had been divorced and a single mother long before that was the norm, long before child care, and before women teachers were paid the same as men. She was the first feminist I ever met, though I doubt she would have called herself one.

In our class, a fourth-form class, students were still forced to endure the ordeal of going around the room reading from our set texts. The humiliation of this for slow readers and torture for fast readers is unthinkable these days. I would cringe at the weak reading skills of others, and be equally angry that I had to waste my time like this, having usually already read the book in the holidays. Once I was reading a book she had loaned me – *The Second Sex*, in fact – behind my class text, and when it was my turn to read aloud was caught out. When she realised what I was reading she made a wry comment, and passed to the next student but with a look in her steely blue eyes that said, *Don't ever do that again*, and I did not. I probably did not appreciate the significance of her giving me books to read; that it meant she recognised in me something of herself.

When I was a child, reading was the only thing I was really good at. On reflection, I excelled at it. But no one ever rewarded this skill, this passion, and no one nurtured it until I was much older. On the contrary, my reading habit was considered obsessive, eccentric and even unhealthy: it would ruin my eyesight, give me bad posture and make me antisocial. And books were always being denied or withheld: primary school librarians were forever telling me I couldn't read a certain book 'above' my reading level, as if these would have some corrosive effect. Yet I cannot recall a single book that has ever harmed me in any way.

Perhaps as a consequence I became a defensive reader, hunkering down deeper into the pages than most and squeezing as much out of them as possible. My texts of my early university days are covered in notes and underlinings, to the point that now I cannot read them, and I am amused by the insights I thought profound enough to scribble all over the pages. It would be logical that I re-read my Tennyson thesis before finishing this essay. But I don't want to be reminded of what I suspect is an obsessive dissection of lines and phrases, detailed to the point of being embarrassing. We might have laughed at the remaining guard of old Leavisites left in Sydney, the main battalion having long decamped to Melbourne in what was then, in the late 1970s, a legendary battle of theory and politics (captured in John Docker's *In A Critical Condition*). But we were merely the next generation, still making our way into the forest of literary studies via the well-worn paths of new criticism, which valued the integrity of the text, prioritised close reading, and rewarded the attentive, submissive reader with moral superiority. (Of that, some of the academics were, I knew, firmly convinced.) But when I read Empson's *Seven Types of Ambiguity* I was filled with amazement and dismay in equal parts. It seemed the meaning he could wring out of a Shakespearean sonnet or even a single line of Keats was infinite, but this astonishingly precocious book – it was written when Empson was twenty-two – struck me as clinical. I could admire the connotations he drew from 'mossed cottage trees' but suspected he had never wept over the image of sad-hearted Ruth amid the alien corn.

The first critical word I was properly trained to use, in my senior high school English classes, was 'irony'. We were told what it was (dramatic, Shakespearean, poetic), how to identify it, why it was important. How ironic that here at UTS at the base of the brown-grey pebblecrete Tower, the last word in urban ugly – perhaps the most maligned building in the city, certainly the least poetic of places on the campus – I have this minor epiphany (another critical word we were trained to use). For epiphany it is: a revelation that this moment, in this place, is somehow the culmination of my career. Of all that I am, all that I do as a reader and a writer. It is a conversation, but as I finish the lecture on *Tirra Lirra by the River*, I hear not my voice but those of Nora Porteous, Maggie Smith, Jean Brodie, Sir Lancelot and the Lady herself, half-sick of shadows but despite that joining this endless conversation with books, a conversation that has been conducted for most of my life. And, yes, these books have ruined my eyesight, given me bad posture and probably also made me antisocial.

'Fine words compel her. Fiction teaches her herself. Her own inner complications are wrought in her reading.'

Gail Jones

Eleanor Reads Emma

Gail Jones

'Consciousness . . . is like a big wind.' Jean-Paul Sartre

WHAT IS IT, TO READ?

They are paper wings you fly on. They are spaces of mysterious black on white rarefaction. You travel through air to the last page. You do not actually exist. You are carried along, a kind of symbol, a useless kind of symbol, integrating all that is there, predisposed, overdetermined, to some destination that is both precious and a total nothingness. It is a cunning procedure. Impersonating and depersonating. And you are lost. And you are found. And you have been everywhere and nowhere. Interiority itself is traduced and shanghaied. Think of it: how strange! What a peculiar absorption.

She had about her a capacity for darkness and desolation so that when she read *Madame Bovary* it seemed ineluctably herself. *I am Emma*

Bovary, she might have whispered to the night, her voice soft and serious and dreamy as Flaubert. She felt the force of synonymity. Of character. Of identification. Emma Bovary gazed with her black eyes at her sumptuous wedding feast, at the four roasts of beef and the six chicken fricassées; at the stewed veal and the legs of mutton and the suckling pig and the pork sausages; at the dishes of trembling yellow cream and the confectioner's candies and pies – it was so abundant she was almost nauseated by its itemisation – but for Eleanor, the reader, the marriage was summarised above all in the detail of the Cupid: the little Cupid on a chocolate swing atop the tiered wedding cake. Eleanor saw this most clearly; it swung in her mind. *So this was their marriage. Doomed by a ludicrous accessory.* And then there was the fishmonger, one of their cousins, who thought it a lark to squirt water from his mouth, through the keyhole, and so embarrass Rouault, the father, and assembled other guests; and Madame Bovary, senior, who was out of sorts and miserable because she had not been consulted as to the dress or the arrangements of the feast; and Charles himself, an awkward bridegroom, behaving entirely unsexual. Emma floated through her wedding like one in a dream. Her presence was almost superfluous and certainly less solid than the food.

(Weddings are like this, thought Eleanor: *other people's salacious engorgement. And perhaps to be a bride is to experience some sort of ritualised obliteration, to become just an ambulant dress, a drifting lacy something. Where indeed is Emma Rouault beneath this mountain of food, beneath these indecorous goings-on?)*

No doubt you know Emma Bovary's story. Bored young woman in a blue merino gown, beautiful in her nails (which were pure ivory and almond-shaped) and in the darkness of her eyes (especially so because of the shadowing of her splendid lashes), falls for Charles, visiting doctor, and man of meritorious stolidity. Charles notices that Emma

Rouault bites her lips when she is silent; he notices too the precise shape of her thick wavy chignon and her tortoiseshell eyeglasses that she rests, like a man, between two buttons of her blouse. He notices that her face beneath the parasol is tinted with shifting reflections. He dotes. He is captivated. He sees her loveable particularity. Emma Rouault, on the other hand, cannot see her lover at all; she merely wants to be swept away; it is an idea she dotes on. So Emma weds, and bears a child, and enters those tedious, terrible estrangements that signify unsuitable marriage. She enters the dull grief of misalliance. She discovers the hollows around which spouses learn to bend and distort. In her own house she is strangled and must throw open the windows just to breathe, and every single day consolidates a vague sense of omission. Yet Emma knows from her reading that there exists a life of passion – she has read of ardent arousal and the mad intensities of love – and so takes lovers and spends money with a kind of desperate extravagance. In the end, disappointed and ruined, her particular beauty eroded, Emma suicides with arsenic. It is a horrible death. And Gustave Flaubert, who as a child watched his father perform dissections on cadavers, is lovingly indelicate in the details he provides.

Our reader's biography is perhaps not so well known. Eleanor Marx, daughter of the more famous and Santa Claus look-alike Karl, is born in London one snowy morning in 1855, the youngest of three surviving sisters. She is, by all accounts, an enchanting child, remarkable for her dark eyes and her sparkling intelligence. Her father's favourite (but not her mother's), Eleanor grows up to become, not unpredictably, a radical socialist. With her small round eyeglasses and her long flowing cape she stands on platforms from Manchester to Chicago denouncing the evils of industrial capitalism and recommending workers' control. Her voice is full and plangent. Workers unite in their applause. She is a heroine of incipient Marxism and nothing at all, it must be added, like the bourgeois and stay-at-home Emma Bovary. But beyond this public life, when she sits beneath a green illuminated lamp under the dome of the British Library, when she is turning pages and moving away on her own private word-fuelled transportation (she thinks of herself elongated, uninhibited, leaning into an invisible, dark wind-tunnel), it is literature Eleanor Marx specifically adores. Fine words compel her. Fiction teaches her herself. Her own inner complications are wrought in her reading. Eleanor loves Shakespeare and Ibsen and Gustave Flaubert; and then she falls for Edward Aveling, well-known cad and gasbag and unconscienced borrower of monies. She dotes on his hands and the way ink stains rest in their filigreed creases; she is captivated by the sunburst irises in his melancholy-looking eyes; and the deep sound of his voice; and his face closed on itself as he sleeps. Those mauve-coloured crescents beneath his eyes. The tiny shadows of his lashes. Edward is not, as it happens, free legally to wed (since he is still married to Isabel Frank, whom he long ago deserted), but Eleanor loves him and they live in London as man and wife. All in all they are together for fourteen years, a period during which Eleanor completes and publishes the first English translation of *Madame Bovary*, and becomes both more beloved of her public and more exhausted by Aveling's obloquy. Eleanor suicides, with prussic acid, at the age of forty-three. Her short obituary in *The Times* does not register any details.

But let us begin elsewhere.

She is thirty-one and impoverished when the translation is undertaken. She is installed in the world-historical name of Marx – a name not yet, however, elevated to the exemplary and the formulaic – and burdened by the inheritance of her father's papers which, three years after his death, she is still ordering with Engels. She spends much of each day reading and writing, engaged in tracing references for the English translation of *Das Capital*. She also composes tracts on 'The Woman Question' and the conditions of child workers labouring their lives away in factories. She researches in the library, and then she teaches Shakespeare to small groups of beribboned frilly girls, twelve lessons – with readings by all members of the class – for one pound one shilling. And somewhere in the midst of this scholarly industry Eleanor Marx reads and translates Gustave Flaubert's *Madame Bovary.*

What is it, then, to read?
What does it mean to enact, irrevocably, even one single sentence?
What is the nature of the presumption of even one single adjective?
The supposition of any syntax?
The ontology of pronouns?

When Eleanor first reads *Madame Bovary* she participates – imagine it – in a sense of compelling extenuation. It is not just the peculiar gratifications of realism – all those plausible details, that named food, those eyelashes, the hairpins placed, during adulterous lovemaking, under the marble pedestal of a clock; it is as though her own ordinary world has grown instantly more substantial. She looks around her bedroom with novelistic vision. Tiny objects are newly exact and radiantly meaningful. Edward's daytime hat, there, askew on the hatstand. A letter on the bureau, in Engels' neat, fussy handwriting. A draped shawl that had been her mother's (paisley and in tones of crimson, threadbare, *mother-shaped*). Piles of scattered miscellaneous books, and a black ribbon at the end of one of them. A brocade curtain slightly blowing, its fringe like eyelashes or a fan. Alone in their double bed – since Aveling has gone into the windy London night and is out somewhere, womanising – Eleanor sees through the intensity of her loneliness that everything is Flaubertian. It is a quality that inheres, she conjectures, in some particular combination of fatigue and detail. *A life smaller than one is.* A world of things, named things, as encumbering and debilitating as they are utterly special and delectable. *I am Emma Bovary*, Eleanor thinks to herself, *I simulate her yearning; I long for the sweet and discriminate engulfments of the amorous. I would, like Emma Bovary, run distressed through a field of oxen driven only by the force of tears and rejection. But then,* she reconsiders, *I am also Charles Bovary. I am besotted. I am foolish. I am unreciprocated. I am work-enclosed and over-diligent and possess meritorious stolidity. And what I feel for Edward Aveling is like words written on the wind.*

When Edward arrives home very late Eleanor is still wide awake, reading. He swings into the room as though blown, his face blotched and pallid with moonlight. The air around him is masculine and smells of brandy. His eyes, which look tired, are slitted and unbeautiful.

'Ah, Gustave Flaubert!' Edward Aveling exclaims; and he leans clumsily onto the bed, plucks the novel from Eleanor's hands, and takes up, somewhat theatrically, the pose of a dandy: legs crossed, a finger to the chin, the book held ridiculously high. He opens at random and reads in execrable French:

> She wore an open dressing-gown, that showed under the shawl-shaped collar a pleated blouse with three gold buttons. Her belt was a corded girdle with great tassels, and her small wine-red slippers had a large knot of ribbon that fell over her instep. She had bought herself a blotter, writing-case, pen-holder, and envelopes, although she had no one to write to she dusted her shelf, looked at herself in the mirror, picked up a book, and then, dreaming between the lines, let it drop on her knees. She longed to travel or to go back to her convent. She wanted to die, but she also wanted to live in Paris.

'What a fop!' Edward giggles. 'La-di-dah women's clothes!'

He tilts his head and repeats in singsong mockery: 'A pleated blouse with three gold buttons.'

Eleanor reaches out gently and hooks the collar of Edward's shirt. He falls backwards into her lap, the book splaying open on his belly.

'You are drunk, my darling. Why don't you come to bed?'

(Upside down his face is still the face that she loves. She would kiss the inverted crescents that frame his melancholy-looking eyes.)

But Edward simply groans and rolls over her, suddenly exhausted, and without removing any of his clothes falls immediately asleep.

This is such a common form of suffering, to be awake, late at night, in an alienated partnership. It is like reading a book oneself has long ago written.

'She wanted to die, but she also wanted to live in Paris.'

Eleanor's book has fallen to the floor and closed its French pleasures. She extinguishes the lantern and lies quietly, listening to the wind. A detonation of pigeon wings momentarily startles her; then it is the black wind again, blowing all around the planet, blowing across the English Channel, furrowing the dark cold water, heading eastwards, and billowing, and rising to a gale.

In the darkness our reader envisions a pair of small wine-red slippers.

During the weeks of translation the novel exists as hallucination. As Eleanor seeks fastidiously each precise and accurate world, the world of Emma does not, as it happens, fade into lexical deliberation or systems of practical vocabulary. Instead it seems now doubly present and doubly actual. Indeed she holds this other life in constant regard: it is the companionable phantasm that daily attends her; it is the vague false memory she internally bears; it is the centring and decentring and radical off-centring of each day. When she is not actually at work, with the two texts before her, Eleanor nevertheless experiences little glimpses and sepia-toned recursions. As she drinks her coffee in the morning she recalls, quite irrelevantly, Emma mechanically spinning a gauzy lampshade decorated with clowns and tightrope walkers as her first love, Leon, reads verses in a low voice. She thinks of the phrenology head Leon gives Charles Bovary as a birthday present; and the cactus he presents to Emma ('a novel having made the mania for cactuses fashionable'). This is a kind of materialism Eleanor

Marx has never considered before: the symbolic life of objects, their clandestine economies, their secret exorbitance. (She wonders what theory-of-value they might possibly apply.)

When the translation is finished, *Madame Bovary* still ghosts Eleanor Marx's inner life. In her reduplicating labour she has come to know the novel too well: it is like falling in love. And when one is in love – is this not so? – bizarre metonymies govern; all details are amatory; everything inevitably *refers*. This is how it seems to Eleanor. Everything in her life refers to Emma.

It is impossible to contemplate the suicide by poison of Eleanor Marx without supposing that, in her extremity and unalleviated misery, she may have recalled the suicide by poison of Emma Bovary.

A few months before her death, Mr Edward Aveling, using a false name, false age and false address, had secretly married a pregnant young woman at the Chelsea Register Office. He may have eventually told Eleanor, or she may have suspected: we do not know. He may also have misappropriated union funds: Eleanor writes to her friends, obliquely and without details, of some kind of 'utter disgrace' she cannot quite bring herself to divulge. Edward Aveling may even have murdered Eleanor Marx: certainly some English socialists believed this was so, and inquest reports, which rehearsed this possibility, were destroyed in the Blitz and are lost forever. In any case Aveling lived only four months after Eleanor's death, and died despised.

And here is Eleanor, poisoned. Ending where all stories end.

It would be comforting to allude to some neat convergence of symbols – that Eleanor thinks, for example, of the Cupid on the wedding cake, that she clothes herself in the crimson mother-shaped shawl, that she kisses a photograph of her father or clutches the new English text of *Madame Bovary* – but death is no multi-dimensioned or novelistic epiphany; it is cruel effacement; it eradicates details. Eleanor convulses on her lonely double bed with the effects of prussic acid. Her breathing is spasmodic and tight, as though she is drowning in air. She is seized by an unspeakable and unwritable agony. Her face turns blue; her muscles paralyse; then death occurs. The atmosphere around her carries the scent of bitter almonds. Pages flap somewhere: a window has been left open. Wind, eerie wind, wreathes its way through the house, giving everything the appearance of an infinitesimal quivering, as though nothing is quite still but the prone body of the dead woman.

When we read of this death it is both real and unreal; it is still and it trembles.

What is it then, to read? What is this death of Eleanor Marx, made up wholly of alphabets?

It is like words written on wind. A kind of dreaming between lines. It is a rarefaction. And it is untranslatable.

'In books, she was carving out a new place to be: a place all her own, where the rest of us could not follow.'

Catherine Keenan

A Native in the Land of Reading

Catherine Keenan

OF ALL THE EVERYDAY MIRACLES AS A CHILD GROWS up, the one that felled me was watching my daughter learn her letters. She went to school for the first time last year; aged five, she was both terrified and eager. Mostly the eagerness won out, but occasionally the size of the task in front of her was overwhelming. Figuring out the curve of an 'a' or the swoop of an 'm' could be so frustrating it made her scream. She would throw down her pencil and declare the task hopeless. It felt to her, and sometimes me, that she was getting nowhere; that those squiggles would forever remain an impenetrable code.

Until, just like that, the world cracked open. The squiggles suddenly formed themselves into words, then sentences, then rolling paragraphs. Soon whole stories unfolded, revealing worlds she never dreamt existed. She left behind the banality of home readers and plunged into real books: books about fairies, girls' schools, detectives, talking animals, mice who love ballet, spies, and magical trees. She read constantly, from the moment she woke until she fell asleep at night, her lamp still on, the hard covers of a dozen or more books poking into her resting limbs. She read with her eyes wide, incredulous at the riches unfurling before her. The size of her world – her sense of what was possible – expanded with every turning page, and she became addicted to what might be made known to her next. Watching her, I sometimes felt a bolt of sadness, the realisation that through her reading she was drifting from me. In books, she was carving out a new place to be: a place all her own, where the rest of us could not follow.

Now, when we have an argument, she doesn't scream with frustration. She stares at me with fury in her eyes, then stomps purposefully up the stairs to her bedroom. She returns with short, heavily-lettered notes expressing her complaints. 'It was NOT my fault!' Or: 'It's not fair – you always take his side.' Or, when she's particularly miffed: 'You don't love me.' She slams the notes down on the bench, and glares at me silently. When I open my mouth, she stamps her foot again and thrusts the pen and paper towards me.

I must not speak my response. I must write it.

~

My daughter looks like me – people comment on it all the time – but what makes us most similar is that when I was her age, I read like that too.

I grew up in Perth in the 1970s, when everything happened outdoors. In our neat suburb, in our closed and happy community, anything that mattered was done in the glare of the belting sun. I can picture, if I try, the inside of our house on Inverness Crescent, but what comes first is the outside: low slung and wide, with a red-brick fence along the front that even the smallest of us could jump over. The hours after school were spent leaping over that wall as we raced into the house for food, then back out to rejoin friends.

Across the road was a triangular plot of land that kept three intersecting roads apart, though the roads were so little used it seemed unnecessary, even then. There was a Chinese apple tree planted on it, and I remember the sour crunch when you bit into the fruit; you'd only eat them if you were starving or had been dared to. My brother and sister and I passed this tree dozens of times a day, riding our bikes in packs. We sailed with our legs held out down the curve to the brown-green expanse of park to play chasey. We puffed our way up to the Porters', whose noticeably bigger, better-appointed house made the lives they lived there seem more vivid. Our primary school was all the way on the other side of the suburb, miles and miles away, it seemed, at the far reach of everything we knew. We didn't ride there, we walked, scuffing our brown school shoes reluctantly along the footpath in the unrelenting heat.

Sport was the rhythm of our lives. It was the thing that connected people and it was assumed, without anyone ever declaring it, to occupy great swathes of every young person's time. Even mine. I was a skinny, pale kid, devoid of any natural abilities, but this didn't spare me from tennis every Saturday, nor the seasonal torture of netball, hockey and tee-ball, nor the endless games of rubbish-bin cricket, me watching helplessly as the ball sailed into the branches of the Chinese apple.

I have many happy memories from that time: memories of picnics at Kalamunda and of warming up after a cold swim at Inglewood Pool by lying belly down on the sun-blasted concrete. But the more immediate memories are of being dumped by waves at Yanchep beach and spinning underwater till my lungs screeched. Or of peeling off my sunburnt skin in sheets, like filo pastry, and watching them float down to the sandy floor. I remember the humiliation of being the last person picked for every one of those sporting teams, and struggling in behind even the chubby kids in school running races. I remember a persistent feeling that this world of sun and action was profoundly not for me. But what else was there?

There was reading. Reading was how I soared away from that life of sunshine and sport; how I leapt over those small humiliations and landed somewhere safe. Our house was not bookish, but there were always a few novels on the shelves. I remember the rows of my parents' fat soft-covers, and the particular thrill of the ones with silver embossed titles. Given the choice, I mostly read Enid Blyton and girls' mysteries: Nancy Drew, Trixie Belden. When those ran out, the Hardy Boys. When those ran out, I read my brother and sister's baby books, if that's all I could get my hands on. At a terrible pinch I read catalogues. Occasionally I was daring enough to sneak down an adult book; the first illicit thrill I remember in my life was reading Jeffrey Archer, equal parts terrified and excited by all that I didn't understand. I read any fiction that fell into my lap; hundreds and hundreds of books, most of which have left not a single trace in my memory.

I had no sense of literary appreciation, and there was no book that changed me. I was an indiscriminate reader because it wasn't the details of plot or character that interested me; it was the fact that a book – any book – could induce in me a concentration so intense it sucked me completely out of my life. Reading created a place I experienced physically, as a new land opened up in my head; an alternate reality I could whoosh off to at any time. The worlds created by each book were different, but they became one: each story was just new territory added to an ever-expanding continent in my mind. Being in any corner of that land washed me with relief, mostly because it felt like this was a place I truly belonged. I fitted awkwardly into my own life, but I was a native in the land of reading.

It was here, in this land, that the most intense moments of my childhood were lived. My days were mostly the same: walking to school, riding around after it, meeting the usual kids at the park. But in the land of reading, wild and unpredictable things happened all the time. I was cracking mysteries and running away from villains. I explored new worlds and tried on new selves. I experimented with emotions I only half understood and experienced the alluring weightlessness of slipping the moorings of myself. Stories gave me the opportunity to tunnel into myself, and in that murky, solitary place I often felt more alive than in any other part of my life. Reading gave me my first inkling of the private self, of the fact that there could be whole worlds in a person's head that no one else could access or disturb. It made me aware of how deep a person could run.

There are differing views about the value of such indiscriminate reading. Novelist Neil Gaiman applauded it in his Reading Agency lecture in 2013, arguing there is no such thing as a bad book for young people. Children should read whatever they like, because each book makes the child a better reader, and better readers seek out better books, and ultimately become better citizens. Novelist Tim Parks argues the contrary: that Harry Potter is not a gateway drug to Shakespeare, and that reading dross most often leads only to reading more dross.

It's true that for me, I didn't come to good books for a long time. It was not until many years later, when I was in upper high school studying literature, that I read my first good book. Indeed, that was the first time I realised books could be divided into categories of good and bad. I still think that if I had never met F. Scott Fitzgerald and e. e. cummings, I would have kept reading Nancy Drew, or her grown-up equivalent, and been perfectly happy. But I did meet Fitzgerald and cummings and I knew instinctively that the land they could add to the continent in my mind was more fertile and expansive than anything that had been added before. Soon I was on to Thomas Hardy and the Brontës and, yes, Shakespeare. As I got older, this led to Virginia Woolf and Tim Winton and Gabriel García Márquez. On my bedside table now sit books by David Mitchell, Marilynne Robinson, Colm Tóibín and Hilary Mantel. It has been many years since I read anything with embossed silver lettering on the cover.

These books – the good books – have taught me many things. They have taught me the infinite complexity of people and intentions, and introduced me to ideas I would never have conjured on my own. They have given me years of variegated pleasure and laid down treasured corners in that wide land in my mind. But it was those early books – the bad books – that taught me the most valuable lessons I have drawn from reading. Bad books were my first window into other worlds and other lives, and they revealed two things: how arbitrary was the life of sunshine and sport around me; and that I would one day leave it behind. Books made it easier when I was overlooked again for the sporting team, and they lent an elegiac quality to those downhill bike rides late on a hot afternoon. The point is not that Nancy Drew led me to Shakespeare, but that she led me to a whole different life.

I know Gracie, too, is a native in the land of reading because she writes notes when she's upset. When she is torn about by blasts of feeling – by fury or fear or any of the inchoate emotions that rip through her seven-year-old body – it feels to her like one of the complex, outsized emotions that belong to that private world of the written word. For her, as for me, that's where the most intense experiences occur, where life is at its most vivid. She writes notes because words are how she is used to understanding the most complex parts of herself.

The joy of watching Gracie read now, as indiscriminate as I was, is the joy of watching her discover these same things. It's the thrill of seeing her explore new worlds from the safety of our couch; of noticing her eyes change as she realises that the way things are is not how they have to be. I can't actually see her trying on emotions and experimenting with ideas and selves, as it all takes place in the private world that reading has created for her. But I know it's going on, because it went on there for me too. I do feel, at times, that her absorption in stories is taking her away from me. But then I remember that the place they are taking her to is a place we'll always belong to together.

'Books . . . have always represented the opportunity to take a walk on the wild side. To leave the comfortable, well-ordered confines of normality and go to where the wild things are.'

Andy Griffiths

Snip! Snap! Snip! Or, Merry Stories and Funny Pictures: How Reading Shaped My Writing

Andy Griffiths

AS A WRITER OF FUNNY BOOKS FOR CHILDREN, I consider it incredibly good fortune that my grandmother owned a copy of the German children's classic *Der Struwwelpeter* – a book of rhyming cautionary tales with the subtitle 'Merry stories and funny pictures'.

'The Dreadful Story of Harriet and the Matches' begins with a mother warning her daughter not to play with matches while she is out of the house. Once alone, however, Harriet wastes no time in playing with the matches, sets her dress on fire and burns to death, ending the story as a smoking pile of ashes being wept over by her two cats.

In 'The Story of Little Suck-a-thumb', a mother warns her son, Conrad, not to suck his thumb while she is out or else the 'long red-legged scissor man' will come in and cut off his thumbs. Like Harriet, Conrad ignores his mother's warning, and, sure enough, a man with long red legs and a gigantic pair of scissors comes in and cuts off his thumbs.

In 'Flying Robert', a young boy always insists on going out walking in stormy weather with his red umbrella and one fateful afternoon gets blown away into the sky, never to be seen again.

Merry stories? Well . . . not really, although the rhymes do have an incongruously cheerful feel to them:

Snip! Snap! Snip! the scissors go;
And Conrad cries out 'Oh! Oh! Oh!'
Snip! Snap! Snip! They go so fast,
That both his thumbs are off at last.

Funny pictures? Not unless you find pictures of burnt, dismembered or 'blown-away' children funny.

An utterly compelling, fascinatingly awful and hilariously horrible introduction to books and the pleasure of reading? You bet.

It's appalling violence, yes, but at the same time, even as a five-year-old I could see that the punishment (or, depending on your point of view, the solution) is out of all proportion to the crime. Sure, Conrad will never suck his thumbs again . . . because he doesn't have any! This discrepancy between the crime and the punishment struck me as quite amusing. The combination of deadpan understatement ('Conrad stands, and looks quite sad, and shows his hands') and brightly coloured pictures creates an absurd surreality that perhaps goes some way to explaining why I was such a sucker for Lewis Carroll's *Alice in Wonderland*, which I encountered soon after.

Nobody ever had to try to persuade me to read. Thanks to *Struwwelpeter* I already knew that *anything* could – and probably would – happen when you turned that page. I was hungry for more, and I couldn't wait to pick up a pen and start my own gruesome imitations. The first recorded instance of my writing is a 'get well' card for my father, which – with the help of a cheery picture of his tombstone – suggested that if he didn't get better soon he would be '*domed*' (I couldn't spell 'doomed'). I was six years old and the fact that he did get better soon afterwards was all the encouragement I needed.

I don't know if Dr Heinrich Hoffman (the author of *Struwwelpeter*) – in his zealous mission to persuade children to listen to the warnings of their parents – realised that he had stumbled onto one of the secrets of writing for children, but he had. Get rid of the parents as quickly as possible and then plunge the child into a world of excitement.

Another of my very favourite authors, Enid Blyton, knew it too. Adults rarely figure in her child-centric books. Whether the kids were on the track of diamond smugglers, flying around in a wishing chair or exploring an enchanted tree, their adventures were always refreshingly and thrillingly adult-free.

Dr Seuss knew it, too. In *The Cat in the Hat* a mother goes out, leaving her two children alone, and an anarchic, fun-loving cat walks in and proceeds to all but destroy the house. And in works of pure nonsense like the sublime *One Fish, Two Fish, Red Fish, Blue Fish*, we don't see any adults at all.

And, of course, the inimitable Roald Dahl certainly knew it. Many of his young heroes and heroines are orphans – either literally or through neglect. In *James and the Giant Peach* Dahl even makes a joke of the fact, by reporting – with a straight face – that James's parents were eaten in London 'in full daylight, mind you, and on a crowded street' by an 'enormous angry rhinoceros' which had escaped from London Zoo.

It wasn't long before I stumbled onto *Hänsel and Gretel*, another tale of children in danger. You might think that parents abandoning their children in a forest is bad enough for one story, but that's only the start. Its attractions for the young reader include gluttony (those kids are so hungry they could eat a house), kidnapping (by a cannibalistic witch), attempted cannibalism (the witch is so hungry she could eat a little boy), enslavement (the witch forces Gretel to help fatten up Hänsel) and murder by oven (well, I guess the old girl had it coming).

The ending of *Hänsel and Gretel* is nominally positive – the children return home with the old woman's treasure and discover that their stepmother is now dead, and they live happily ever after with their father. (It bothered me then, however, as it does now, that the father somehow escapes censure or penalty for his actions.)

It's a story full of horror, yes, but I knew instinctively even as a child that the hero of a story is heroic only in proportion to the challenges he or she faces. Hänsel and Gretel face a dangerous world, but they use their resourcefulness and courage to triumph in a story that is impossible to forget. A writer of stories for children cannot afford to pull his or her punches. If you don't confront your characters with a suitable amount of mayhem, chaos and violence, your readers will go find it elsewhere – in movies, online or in their own made-up games (which are more likely to feature marauding pirates, terrifying monsters and random acts of cruelty than stories of well-adjusted children obeying their loving parents).

Another piece of outrageously good fortune for me as a developing reader was the fact that my mother helped to run the second-hand bookstall at my primary school fete. Each year, for a few months leading up to the fete, our spare bedroom would fill up with dozens of box-loads of donated books that I was free to pore over and explore at my leisure.

I'm pretty sure it was in the spare bedroom that I first encountered the wonderfully subversive and inspirational *How to be Topp: a guide to sukcess for tiny pupils, including all there is to kno about SPACE* by Geoffrey Willans and Ronald Searle. This book is narrated by the irrepressible Nigel Molesworth – a student at St Custards Grammar who enjoys an active fantasy life and is possibly the world's worst speller.

There were also numerous copies of E. W. Cole's amazing *Cole's Funny Picture Books*, which were even more comprehensive explorations of the wild kingdom that *Struwwelpeter* had opened up for me.

Another of my favourites from this period was *The Magic Power of Your Mind*, a 1940 self-help book that asserted that our minds are far more powerful than we suspect and it's worth spending a bit of time exploring how they work and how we can make better use of them. I was already developing a great passion for fiction and absurd humour, and this book triggered a life-long interest in works of psychology and philosophy. (And don't get me started on the psychology and philosophy of humour . . .)

The school fete also proved fortuitous because aside from the second-hand bookstall my other favourite place to hang out was the White Elephant stall. It was here that I paid 40 cents for a 1920s Underwood typewriter. After somehow managing to carry it home (those things are heavy!), I borrowed a Pitman's 'Teach Yourself to Type' book from the library and dutifully taught myself to type without looking at the keys. Soon I was typing out passages and entire chapters from my favourite books – a practice I've since discovered is recommended by many writers as a way of really getting inside a text and figuring out how it works.

Another early – and intensely important – reading experience for me was American horror and science-fiction comics of the early 1970s. These were readily available in the general store of the caravan park we used to holiday at every summer, and featured well-told stories of ghouls, aliens, mad professors and even madder monsters. I spent many happy – and slightly terrifying – afternoons in my orange nylon tent lost in these *Twilight Zone*-style fantasies. (I still get a great deal of pleasure from them and marvel at the sheer economy of the storytelling in the fast-moving tales.)

One of my favourite stories, called 'Monsters of the Mind', told of an alien who – in an effort to discover the state of the Earth's defences against alien invasion – disguises himself as a diplomat called John Restin. But after a severe blow to the head, he forgets that he's an alien and imagines he really *is* a diplomat called John Restin, who identifies with humanity rather than his alien brotherhood. It's complicated, but for some reason this story really struck a chord and left me wondering how anybody could be truly and absolutely confident they were really who they thought they were. (It wasn't until many years later that I encountered Alan Watts's seminal distillation of Eastern philosophy, *The Book: On the Taboo Against Knowing Who You Are*, and realised that greater minds than mine have grappled with this question throughout the ages.)

Another story, 'What was "X": the Thing that Lived!' dramatised the dilemma of Charles Bentley, a comic writer whose quest to create the ultimate indestructible monster results in him creating 'X'. The monster has the capability to evade all attempts by the US army, navy and air force to obliterate it by shapeshifting itself into whatever form will render the attack harmless. If you drive a tank at it, it becomes a wall of diamond. Fire a bazooka shell and it becomes a puff of smoke. Bentley's story is a huge hit, but then he is mortified to discover that his creature *has* actually come to life, and is not only wreaking havoc but is every bit as indestructible as described in his comic.

Bentley finally realises that 'X' lives as a result of having been typed up on a mysterious typewriter he found in an antique shop and the only way to destroy 'X' – who is coming after him in the same way that Frankenstein's monster turned on its creator – is to destroy the typewriter by throwing it out of the window.

Okay, I recognise there are strong parallels here, but as far as I know none of the creatures that I dreamt up on my Underwood typewriter have subsequently taken on a life of their own. However, I am confident that judging by my numerous encounters with – and letters from – enthusiastic readers over the years, I've been successful in creating books that come alive for them in the same way that the books I loved came alive for me and inspired my love of reading.

From *Struwwelpeter*, Enid Blyton and American horror comics it was a relatively easy jump – via *Mad* magazine and the short stories of Ray

Bradbury (*The Illustrated Man*) and Roald Dahl (*Kiss, Kiss*) – to Franz Kafka's sublime novella *The Metamorphosis*.

The first line of *The Metamorphosis* reads, 'As Gregor Samsa awoke one morning from uneasy dreams he found himself transformed in his bed into a gigantic insect.' The first line of *The Day My Bum Went Psycho* reads: 'Zack Freeman woke out of a deep sleep to see his bum perched on the ledge of his bedroom window.'

Coincidence? Or clumsily bowdlerised homage?

Obviously the latter, but the utterly matter-of-fact way that Kafka relates the surreal tragicomic dilemma of Gregor Samsa's inexplicable transformation into a gigantic insect both stunned and delighted my fifteen-year-old self and gave me a big clue about how to write humour (i.e. narrate outrageously improbable events with a completely straight face and in a reassuringly reasonable tone).

It is this approach that I have always instinctively used when telling stories. I grew up in a neighbourhood filled with young children and one of my favourite pastimes was telling them apparently true but quite outrageously silly stories and seeing just how far I could take them before the kids stopped believing me. For instance, a small cut on my hand became incontrovertible evidence of a titanic struggle with a shark in the bath that morning. A hand-drawn skull and crossbones on my arm would become proof that my family and I were secretly pirates. Every time my young listener requested more information or challenged me on a point of logic or probability, it would force me to invent more supporting detail and become even more creative. It was a game of 'Let's Pretend' for both myself and the child in which we effectively collaborated to create the story.

I consider my books to be a written extension of this game. *Let's pretend* that bad is good and good is bad (The Bad Books). *Let's pretend* that bottoms can detach themselves from your body and run away (*The Day My Bum Went Psycho*). And, hey, while we're at it, *let's pretend* that my long-serving/suffering illustrator Terry Denton and I are a pair of irresponsible idiots living in an ever-expanding fantasy treehouse existing on a diet of marshmallows and lemonade while we battle a variety of foes, including sea monsters, giant gorillas, headless pirates, vengeance-seeking vegetables and malfunctioning machines in our never-ending quest to deliver our next book to our mean publisher before the deadline . . . Oh, hang on . . . that's real life . . . (well, at least the bit about us being irresponsible idiots battling to meet our deadlines).

For me, books – both reading and writing them – have always represented the opportunity to take a walk on the wild side. To leave the comfortable, well-ordered confines of normality and go to where the wild things are. And not only to play with the wild things but to go inside their minds. To *become* a wild thing. And to become a wild thing so completely and utterly that, when you shut the book, you have totally forgotten you ever laboured under the delusion that you were a human being.

'What I have valued most is the sense of company these authors give me; a sense of a whole history of forms, language, and ideas that I might have a conversation with in my own work.'

Delia Falconer

‘This Stuff Tastes of Window’: Reading as a Writer

Delia Falconer

IN SEPTEMBER 2014, AT THE NEW ZEALAND POST BOOK Awards ceremony, New Zealand author Eleanor Catton announced that she was setting up a grant with her winnings to give writers ‘time to read’. Already the youngest winner of the £50,000 Booker Prize for *The Luminaries*, the twenty-eight-year-old writer dedicated her $15,000 prize money – for the best fiction and people’s choice awards – to giving other writers ‘the means and opportunity not to write, but to read, and to share what they learn through their reading with their colleagues in the arts’. She called the grant the Horoeka/Lancewood Reading Grant, a reference to the horoeka, or lancewood, a native tree that ‘begins its life defensively, with sharp, rigid leaves and a narrow bearing, and at a certain point transforms into a shape that is confident, open and entirely new – so different, in fact, that the young and old versions of the tree look absolutely unalike. That is what I believe that reading can do.’

There is no doubt in my mind that Catton is right. I have been teaching creative writing since 1995 – since I began to have some success as a writer myself – though I have never taken a creative writing course. Instead, as an arts student, I enrolled in a very traditional four-year English degree. Somewhat like a visit to the Louvre, or the Hermitage, it was a hasty march through the treasures of English-language writing, from Spenser's *Faerie Queene* and Milton's *Paradise Lost*, via the Romantic poets, through to Eliot's *The Waste Land* and, joyfully, Flann O'Brien's *At Swim-Two-Birds*. In our final year we studied over sixty works, though English literature, it seemed, stopped at the middle of the twentieth century.

I have no regrets. It was the best training to be a writer, although I did not know this at the time. I came away with a virtual library in my head, almost like one of those ancient Roman memory systems, into which I could slot and sort the books I discovered later. I developed an ear for the sounds and syntax of different eras, which means that I can still place a writer by century by their style alone, and mimic different styles myself. What I have valued most is the sense of company these authors give me; a sense of a whole history of forms, language and ideas that I might have a conversation with in my own work. They have remained a source of comfort, not intimidation. I have always loved Eudora Welty's response in a *Paris Review* interview when asked about writing in a South dominated by the work of William Faulkner. It was 'like living near a big mountain, something majestic – it made me happy to know it was there, all that work of his life'. Besides, she said, she did not think of Faulkner when she was writing, but when she *read*.

When I think back to my early twenties, to that time of still-innocent reading, it seems I learnt just as much from my fellow students. It was my friends who introduced me to Gabriel García Márquez, Jeanette Winterson, Milan Kundera and Bruce Chatwin, who would each have an enormous impact in forming a young woman who was still a reader, not yet a writer. At the time the Picador spinner and the Penguin Classics shelves in bookstores were reliable sources for discovering exciting work, especially by minor writers, such as Jules Laforgue (one of my early loves). The still-browsable shelves of the University of Sydney's library were another education, where I was as likely to pick up Čapek as Chaucer. And surely one's early years of reading are as much about the minor as the major; the greater torrent of books from which the classics have emerged. I never much liked Arnold Bennett when we studied him, but when a friend my age who grew up in Melbourne describes it as the world's last Victorian city – 'like something out of Bennett' – it is important to me that we both know exactly what this means. Perhaps it's the minor work – in my case, Lawrence Durrell's quartet, quintet and travel writing; *The Desire and Pursuit of the Whole* by the mad Baron Corvo; Rilke's notebooks; the Blaise Cendrars given to me by a boyfriend – that most connects us to the literary impulse in its raw, and most bewitching, state. There is also the comforting knowledge, in those less than perfect works, that a book may prove worthy of its existence with just one brilliant concept or blazing sentence. I believe it is these little hits of extraordinary prose the true reader is always reading for, and which she treasures, even more than the most perfectly formed story.

But what does it mean to read, as a writer? While we might read, and re-read, for a sense of the greater architecture of a novel (or a story), it is in the shining moment – the odd catch of a phrase or action – that we perhaps most learn our craft. And it is in this accumulation of remembered moments that one's own writing begins. I am vague now on the plot of Jeanette Winterson's *The Passion*, but I still retain the impact (almost physical) of the early, repeated incantation, 'I am telling you stories. Trust me', along with the fact that one of its two main characters is Napoleon's personal chef, whose sole job is to roast the emperor's chickens. These were revelations. For the first time it struck me that it was entirely possible to write out of a different genealogy – English literature's connection with a lyric, oral past. (And now, at once, I find myself thinking of my favourite line from Sir Thomas Malory's *Le Morte d'Arthur*: Lancelot and Guinevere meet, and 'they loved togidyrs more hotter than they ded toforehonde'.) Prose rhythm carries its own erotic charge – something another of my most-loved, now less-remembered writers, John Ruskin, also understood in his own repressed way, for every ounce of his virginal energy goes into building Victorian cadences of his mighty sentences. I realised something else too, reading Winterson: history did not need to be expressed in the novel through the interminable epic canvases of Sir Walter Scott (definitely not a favoured minor author, except in a cautionary sense). Rather, history could express itself in the way a character cooks, or has sex, or ties a shoelace. I have been too scared to return to *The Passion*, as Winterson's other work has lost its magic for me, but I love it still for tuning my ear to the incantatory and lyric. It ignited the joy I still find in John Banville's *The Untouchable* or E. L. Doctorow's *Ragtime*. (How I adore those beautiful, yet comically balanced, opening sentences: 'Tennis racquets were hefty and the racquet faces elliptical. There was a lot of sexual fainting.')

It was wonderful to really start my reading life in the 1980s, as the 'new exotics' turned the novel into something astonishing and unfamiliar. There was another lesson in Bruce Chatwin's *In Patagonia*: you could dispense with long pages of description – our inheritance from the Victorians – and simply cherrypick the most odd or arresting detail. His were books as distillation, not expansion. Márquez, too, was galvanising. First, he showed me that metaphor could run deeper than comparisons within a sentence: instead, magical events could stand in for whole historical processes, or emotions. A ghost might feel so lonely it refused to leave a village. Love might manifest as a great flock of butterflies, thickening the air. Again, a very specific moment holds all of Márquez for me. In *Love in the Time of Cholera*, as Dr Juvenal Urbino begins to feel the undertow of old age, he declares of his camomile tea, 'This stuff tastes of window.' What sentence could better convey the first horrific slip down the rabbit-hole of dementia? This is the greatest thing I have ever learnt about writing as a reader: that one atypical detail can hold more force than pages of description – and one perfect phrase of speech more than whole conversations. I realise now that I first recognised the special magic of the atypical, without knowing it, as a teenager, when I was struck by Charles Dickens' characterisation of Tommy Traddles in *David Copperfield*. Young Tommy is the kind of plump boy teachers love to hit; his great hobby is drawing skeletons. When he is beaten, the only way the boy knows to channel his loneliness and grief is to pour dozens of these bony companions out onto the page. I have never forgotten him.

Other great discoveries . . . The enduring power of a perfect line: Gatsby, about to kiss Daisy for the first time, seems to hear 'the tuning-fork that had been struck upon a star'. Michael Ondaatje, in *Coming Through Slaughter*, throwing a jazz riff across a page – 'Passing wet chicory that lies in the field like the sky' – with nothing but blank space around it, proving that space is as much a part of any piece of writing as its words. The grand, immersive experience of my favourite novel, *Moby-Dick*. While a short story or novella can seek perfection, I have realised through all my readings of Melville's masterpiece that a novel is instead given life by bagginess – by the illusion that its world is so big it partly eludes its author's grasp. ('Give me a condor's quill! Give me a Vesuvius' crater for an ink stand!')

I first read the novel just after leaving university (because American fiction, along with Australian, also fell beyond the limits of my course). To create its own language – in this instance, a heightened Victorian-American English – would seem thereafter to me a novel's noblest aim. I have since realised that Melville achieved something else: a perfect narrative machine, so deeply rooted conceptually and metaphorically, so structurally open, that it could conceivably be extended forever. My love for the novel above all other literary forms springs almost entirely from this understanding.

Joan Didion famously typed out pages of Hemingway, as if doing a dance with hands on keys that would allow her to absorb the rhythms of his sentences. I have, in turn, read and re-read (and copied out) Joan Didion – just as I have obsessively revisited Helen Garner's writing, trying to understand what makes her implacable sentences so addictive. But this isn't about imitation – even Didion's retyping. Instead, the writer as reader is always approaching writing as a mystery. For all that one might know, theoretically, about grammar or technique, writing's endless fascination is the way everything can shift on a punctuation point, or the placement of two words. Then there is the even more enduring inscrutability of a writer's unique voice, or (such a felicitous phrase) their 'petite musique'. While another writer's style is so plainly theirs, it is my experience, at least, that my own remains enigmatic to me, that, as Montaigne realised in the 1500s, I write to put myself together, to 'discover' who I am, in the process of the writing. Reading other writers' voices is reassuring and inspiring, and part of the alchemical process of coming into one's own style. In some ways, reading for voice reminds me of those years I spent, as I entered adolescence, consuming biographies and autobiographies obsessively. One's writing voice is also a kind of second life, and it helps to see how others have lived theirs.

Lately, I have noticed a new phenomenon: 'bibliotherapy'. At popular philosopher Alain de Botton's School of Life, 'bibliotherapists' in residence sit and talk with the reader about the books they have read and liked in the past and concoct an 'inspirational reading prescription that's tailor-made for you'. This is, of course, also the business of a good independent bookseller. And it is the business of a creative-writing teacher. As a teacher, I 'prescribe' my students reading – lists that are partly about expanding their interests, but are especially about seeing how writers solve certain problems in their prose. Struggling with the biographical portrait of an elusive relative? Let's have a look at Paul Auster's *Invention of Solitude*, a book about his almost pathologically ordinary father, in which the young author narrates with honest precision the very difficulties of the act of writing itself. Let's look closely, again, at that opening paragraph in which he goes through his dead father's drawer, and summons our sympathy and curiosity from this very ordinary array of objects. Some students, I realise, are disappointed by not being given a rule book, or the secrets to prize-winning structure. But there are no short-cuts. Through reading, each writer has to come to his or her own conclusion about what moves them, what they can tolerate, or not. In other words, teaching creative writing is also about training students to read as writers. And yet, I sometimes worry that being given such focus may rob them of an essential element of randomness – that transformative element Catton summons in her image of the horoeka.

Now that writing is my career, I find I am much more likely to read with an eye for solving a particular difficulty, or to see how a writer deals with the challenges of a particular topic. I miss that earlier, undirected reading, which was, without my knowing it, hugely purposeful. I wonder if Catton does too, and that is why she has had the generosity and insight to understand the freedom her grant offers. And yet, I also find myself thinking again of Ondaatje's single, bold line, stretched out across the page, which still exhilarates me. It reminds me there is another reason I read, and it is the constant search for the 'permission' other writers give me. I am always looking for the writer who stretches the limits of the possible in some way, who makes me think, *Yes, it is possible.* And, *Perhaps I can also do that.*

It's this process that Catton seems to be thinking of in her conception of the reading writer as a tree; but I prefer a different image of ingestion and transformation, from Vladimir Nabokov, in an interview with Alvin Toffler in 1964. Although he was speaking about the process of making notes for *Lolita*, he could just as easily have been describing the longer process of reading towards one's writing self. 'All I know,' he said,

> is that at a very early stage of the novel's development I get this urge to garner bits of straw and fluff, and eat pebbles. Nobody will ever discover how clearly a bird visualises, or if it visualises at all, the future of the nest and the eggs in it. What I remember afterwards is the force that made me jot down the correct names of things, or the inches and tints of things, even before I actually needed the information. I am inclined to assume that what I call, for want of a better term, inspiration, had already been at work, mutely pointing at this or that, having me accumulate the known materials for an unknown structure.

'For a seven-year-old who had known nothing but drought – a dry ocean of stubble as far as the eye could reach – the verdant landscape and the Lakeland setting of th[is] book were intoxicating. I went at its pages like a starveling with a cookbook.'

GEORDIE WILLIAMSON

Swallows and Amazons

Geordie Williamson

IN 1977, WHEN I WAS FIVE, MY GRANDFATHER DIED. It came as little surprise – he hadn't been well for a long time – and hurt even less, at least for me. My grandfather was distant in a literal sense. He lived in Scotland, the far side of the world from my family – a vague and genial absence known only from Christmas cards and long-distance phone calls which, back then, had to be booked days in advance. So, I recall no genuine sense of loss at the news. Since I have no legitimate memories to go by, presumably I made some brief, appropriately theatrical display of grief and then got on with refuelling my fleet of Lego spaceships.

It was a few months later that my grandfather returned to us. By which I mean, the contents of his home was packed into containers and shipped twelve and a half thousand miles south. Moving trucks winced over the corrugations of our poorly graded driveway to deliver the accumulated detritus of a sporting estate in the Angus Glens to a drought-ridden farm in central New South Wales.

There were treasures among the moth-eaten plus-fours, Victorian fish-knife sets and trout flies. The head of a stuffed wild cat snarled in perpetuity from its wooden mounting, while a dangerously sharp dagger called a skean dhu was found to have a fork conveniently embedded in its sheath. There were ceremonial swords and walking sticks with handles carved from rams' horns, and even a centuries-old wooden travelling chest known as a vargueno, whose reputed secret compartment my brother and I never did manage to find. Best of all was a small plastic donkey that shat cigarettes when you pulled back its ears.

My fascination with these curios soon faded. Instead, I began haunting the shelves in my father's study, now lined from floor to ceiling with old leather books. There was a time when the family library mainly consisted of paperbacks by Wilbur Smith and Alistair MacLean; now the walls were filled with complete runs of Scott's *Waverley* novels, volumes of Milton's poetry and Carlyle's essays. Not that I had a clue what was in them: I was drawn to the glamour of knowledge that emanated from their collective spines, already beginning to crack in the moistureless heat. In that pre-internet era, they promised a form of total knowledge, closed to me by an ignorance of the code in which they were written.

Although my reading skills improved over the years to the point where I could understand the books' contents, my boredom threshold remained stubbornly low. It didn't help that I tended to choose poorly: dull theological tracts or nineteenth-century volumes on grouse moor maintenance. One day my father must have taken pity on a kid reading furiously out of his depth. From the shelves, he drew a slim volume in green boards, newer than the musty tomes with marbled endpapers, though still deliciously antique-looking to me. *Swallows and Amazons* was written in gilt along the cover. It had me at the title.

Swallows and Amazons was the first book from my grandfather's library I managed to read all the way through, though this is not the achievement it sounds, since it was also one of the few books for children he possessed. It told the story of two bands of young people who spend a holiday camping, sailing, fishing and exploring in England's Lake District. The world described in its pages is almost inconceivable today, so sweet and innocent and evacuated it is of reference to adult ills. Even at the time of its publication in 1930, at the height of the Great Depression, *Swallows and Amazons* presented a fairytale vision of British youth, where the only 'grog' consumed was ginger beer and the greatest threat to the social order was a break-and-enter gang.

Despite (or because of) this, the work was a bestseller. Its author, *Manchester Guardian* journalist Arthur Ransome, went on to write eleven more books in a series that continued the children's adventures, with ongoing commercial success but increasingly unlikely plot lines. Scholars have claimed that Ransome's books changed the course of English literature. They certainly altered the nation's sense of how to spend a holiday – the Lake District became a tourist mecca on the back of the books' success, and generations of kids took to field and hedgerow, boat and river, to replicate those imagined adventures.

I knew none of this when I read the novel. I only knew that I envied the 'Amazons' – John, Susan, Roger and (ahem) Titty Walker – their mock battles and epic picnics with best frenemies Nancy and Peggy Blackett (named like the others for their boat, 'Swallow'). I loved without reservation the adventurousness the kids displayed, a pluck and daring that felt real even as it unfolded in a universe seemingly without sharp edges. For a seven-year-old who had known nothing but drought – a dry ocean of stubble as far as the eye could reach – the verdant landscape and the Lakeland setting of the book were intoxicating. I went at its pages like a starveling with a cookbook.

Flicking through it now, I am ashamed at my credulousness. The prose is no more than workmanlike, and the characters are caught in the rictus of a class system that was already in decay at the time of the book's writing. Like so many once-exemplary texts of British children's fiction, *Swallows and Amazons* replicates in miniature form the ideology of Empire. The experience of re-reading the book is like finding ourselves in a space known to us from childhood as vast and imposing, only to find it unimpressive when viewed on an adult scale.

But if the magic has fled, whose fault is that: Arthur Ransome's or mine? What use the schooled critical intelligence that I (as a full-time book reviewer) supposedly bring to the task of reading, if its ultimate effect is disenchantment? It seems to me that, just like so many things in life, the great undertaking of writing and reading and sorting and grading and teaching and praising that surrounds and bolsters the enterprise known as serious 'literature' is at heart a vain effort to recuperate some of the passion for books we experienced as children. One of my favourite poems by W. H. Auden, 'Atlantis', touches on this paradox:

> Should storms, as may well happen,
> Drive you to anchor a week
> In some old harbour-city
> Of Ionia, then speak
> With her witty scholars, men
> Who have proved there cannot be
> Such a place as Atlantis:
> Learn their logic, but notice
> How its subtlety betrays
> Their enormous simple grief;
> Thus they shall teach you the ways
> To doubt that you may believe.

So, perhaps I should not feel ashamed at my initial love for *Swallows and Amazons* after all. Because reading in childhood precedes questions of taste, value, hierarchy, genre. Indeed, that anarchic openness highlights the vexed nature of contemporary definitions of literature. For a long time, 'literature' consisted of a closed canon of approved books, a secular gospel mainly made up of the works of dead white blokes.

Then came a moment when the academy and the reading public rebelled: the canon was abolished, the better to make room for all kinds of books by all kinds of writers. This broad democracy came with its own virtues (openness to voices that once lay silent on the margins, and a new-found respect for the best genre writing) and vices (that same openness led to the commercial marketplace becoming the arbiter of literary merit: the canon gave way to Amazon's sell-you-more-stuff algorithm), but the change demanded a more expansive idea of what literature *was*. Here is Terry Eagleton's effort to pin it down:

> the term 'literature' operates rather like the word 'weed': weeds are not particular kinds of plant, but just any kind of plant which for some reason or another a gardener does not want around. Perhaps 'literature' means something like the opposite: any kind of writing which for some reason or another somebody values highly.

'As the philosophers might say,' he continues, '"literature" and "weed" are functional rather than ontological terms: they tell us about what we do, not about the fixed being of things.' Though this definition seems too wide for me (surely the degree of intensity, care, or intelligence we bring to the reading experience should add special value to the books we decide to praise), the point makes sense in relation to that little boy lying on a sunbaked verandah with an old-fashioned children's book.

The official 'literary' qualities of the book were not important to me, because I was yet to become aware of the existence of such qualities. Just as Miranda in Shakespeare's play *The Tempest* considers Ferdinand to be a pure spirit of beauty when she first lays eyes on him – shipwrecked for years, she's never seen another man apart from her father – I loved the book because virtually the only others I knew until that point were the age-approved picture books at school. This was my novel (I cracked the code!) and the world it revealed to me proved to be exotic in the extreme, so at variance it was with the environment in which it was read.

Swallows and Amazons set me off on a strange reading path. A little later on, a generous local lady with the imperishable name of Betty Virtue heard I was a mad reader and gifted me a box of decommissioned library books. They also proved to be a batch of early- to mid-nineteenth-century British children's fiction (recall that we barely had a local publishing industry until after World War II), including a 1958 Puffin edition of Edith Nesbit's 1899 novel *The Story of the Treasure Seekers* (a great inspiration to Arthur Ransome, I later learnt) as well as her 1905 classic *The Railway Children*. Nesbit had more humour, more sadness, and a more finely developed social conscience than her later male followers (she was a socialist), and it was through these books and others like them that I finally came to the Narnia sequence of C. S. Lewis.

The residual joy of these books lies in their collective vision of an adult-free universe. Sometimes this is a matter for grief, as in *The Railway Children* (the father in that novel has been accused of selling state secrets and has been taken for questioning). More often, it is a question of benign neglect. The Swallows and Amazons roam free from dawn till dusk (and even after dark); the thoughtless freedom they enjoy is a world away from our panicked and closely policed contemporary parenting. The ecological implications of this shift are more profound than they seem. Entire generations have been cut off from some originary, unmediated knowledge of the natural world. In his forthcoming book on writing and landscape,

Landmarks, English nature writer Robert Macfarlane sets out the phenomenon in stark terms:

> We live in an era of diminishing childhood contact with nature, and landscapes outside the urban. A 2012 'Natural Childhood' report recorded that between 1970 and 2010, the area in which British children were permitted to play unsupervised shrank by 90 per cent. The proportion of children playing regularly in 'wild' places fell from one in two to one in ten. In another study, participants from three generations were given maps of the places in which they grew up, and asked to mark with crosses where they remembered playing. The spread of the crosses – the so-called 'roaming radius' – tightened from generation to generation, until in the third it was cinched right down to house, garden and pavement. Screen-time has increased dramatically. Environmental literacy has plummeted. Nine out of ten children can identify a Dalek; three out of ten a magpie.

But for all its joyful concentration on the ecological imagination in childhood, the only problem with this personal canon was that it spoke of a world elsewhere with such insistence that I came to look on the ground beneath my feet as separate from the world of story. Britain was the place where narrative happened; Australia was a vacancy that required imaginative escape. So it was that, for many years – until I discovered the fiction of Ivan Southall, Colin Thiele and others – I could not synch the world of the imagination with the world around me.

Even still, this bifurcation lingered. I moved to the UK as a postgraduate student and stayed for half a decade, considering that I had finally returned home. It was only after a period in the West Country, and a stirring sense of homesickness, that I picked up an adult work of Australian literature at a second-hand bookstore.

That novel, Martin Boyd's *The Cardboard Crown*, reversed the current of my imagination. It was in an antipodean story, read lying among the cow parsley on the 'undercliff' behind Lyme Regis, that I discovered the landscape I never knew I'd been hungry for.

Reading List

The following is a list of books discussed or mentioned in *The Simple Act of Reading*, as a guide for readers wanting to read more.

Joan Aiken	*The Wolves of Willoughby Chase* (1962)
Louisa May Alcott	*An Old-Fashioned Girl* (1869)
	Little Women (1880)
Jessica Anderson	*Tirra Lirra by the River* (1978)
Thea Astley	*The Well Dressed Explorer* (1962)
W. H. Auden	'Atlantis' (1941)
Jane Austen	*Pride and Prejudice* (1813)
	Northanger Abbey (1818)
Paul Auster	*Invention of Solitude* (1982)
R. M. Ballantyne	*The Coral Island* (1858)
John Banville	*The Untouchable* (1997)
Simone de Beauvoir	*The Second Sex* (1949)

Enid Blyton	*Famous Five* series (1942–63)
	Mary Mouse series (1942–64)
	The Magic Faraway Tree (1943)
	Secret Seven series (1949–63)
Alain de Botton	*The Romantic Movement* (1994)
Martin Boyd	*The Cardboard Crown* (1952)
Ray Bradbury	*The Illustrated Man* (1951)
Phyllis Briggs	*King Arthur and the Knights of the Round Table* (1960)
Charlotte Brontë	*Jane Eyre* (1847)
	Villette (1853)
Dan Brown	*The Da Vinci Code* (2003)
Mary Grant Bruce	*Billabong* series (1910–1942)
Edward Bulwer-Lytton	*The Last Days of Pompeii* (1834)
John Bunyan	*The Pilgrim's Progress* (1678)
Frances Hodgson Burnett	*The Secret Garden* (1911)
Richard Burton	*The Book of the Thousand Nights and a Night [The Arabian Nights]* (1885)
Italo Calvino	*Invisible Cities* (1972)
Truman Capote	*In Cold Blood* (1965)
Gabrielle Carey & Kathy Lette	*Puberty Blues* (1979)
Eric Carle	*The Very Hungry Caterpillar* (1969)
Lewis Carroll	*Alice's Adventures in Wonderland* (1865)
Eleanor Catton	*The Luminaries* (2013)
Benvenuto Cellini	*Autobiography* (1568)
Mollie Chappell	*The Mystery of the Silver Circle* (1955)
Bruce Chatwin	*In Patagonia* (1977)
Edward William Cole	*Cole's Funny Picture Book* (1879)
Susan Coolidge	*What Katy Did* (1872)
	What Katy Did Next (1886)
Susan Cooper	*The Dark is Rising* (1973)
Baron Corvo	*The Desire and Pursuit of the Whole* (1909; 1934)

Roald Dahl	*Kiss, Kiss* (1960)
	James and the Giant Peach (1961)
Luke Davies	*Candy* (1997)
Charles Dickens	*Dombey and Son* (1848)
	David Copperfield (1850)
	A Tale of Two Cities (1859)
	Great Expectations (1860)
John Docker	*In a Critical Condition* (1984)
E. L. Doctorow	*Ragtime* (1975)
Fyodor Dostoyevsky	*Crime and Punishment* (1866)
Alexandre Dumas	*Camille* (1852)
George Eliot	*Middlemarch* (1871–72)
T. S. Eliot	*The Waste Land* (1922)
William Empson	*Seven Types of Ambiguity* (1930)
Gustave Flaubert	*Madame Bovary* (1856)
Helen Fowler	*The Family at Willow Bend* (1955)
Anne Frank	*The Diary of Anne Frank* (1947)
Marilyn French	*The Women's Room* (1977)
Betty Friedan	*The Feminine Mystique* (1963)
Joseph Furphy	*Such Is Life* (1903)
Helen Garner	*Monkey Grip* (1977)
	The Children's Bach (1984)
	True Stories (1996)
	The Spare Room (2008)
Walter M. Germain	*The Magic Power of Your Mind* (1940)
William Golding	*Lord of the Flies* (1954)
Elizabeth Goudge	*The Little White Horse* (1946)
Kenneth Grahame	*The Wind in the Willows* (1908)
Nicholas Stuart Gray	*The Apple Stone* (1965)
Graham Greene	*Ways of Escape* (1980)
	Travels With My Aunt (1969)
Andy Griffiths	*The Day My Bum Went Psycho* (2001)
Thomas Hardy	*The Return of the Native* (1878)

Elizabeth Harrower	*The Watch Tower* (1966)
Anita Heiss	*Sacred Cows* (1996)
	Tiddas (2014)
Xavier Herbert	*Capricornia* (1938)
Hergé (Georges Remi)	*The Adventures of Tintin* (1929–86)
Heinrich Hoffman	*Der Struwwelpeter* (1845)
Homer	*The Iliad* and *The Odyssey*
Chloe Hooper	*The Tall Man* (2008)
Laura Lee Hope	*The Bobbsey Twins* series (1904–79)
Ion Idriess	*The Drums of Mer* (1933)
John Irving	*The World According to Garp* (1978)
Henry James	*The Turn of the Screw* (1898)
Terri Janke	*Butterfly Song* (2005)
Tove Jansson	*The Summer Book* (1972)
James Joyce	*Ulysses* (1922)
	Finnegans Wake (1939)
Franz Kafka	*The Metamorphosis* (1915)
Jack Kerouac	*On the Road* (1957)
Rudyard Kipling	*The Jungle Book* (1894)
Gustav Kobbé	*The Complete Opera Book* (1919)
Harper Lee	*To Kill a Mockingbird* (1960)
Stan Lee & Jack Kirby	'What was "X": The Thing that Lived!' *Marvel Comics* (June 1961)
C. S. Lewis	*The Lion, the Witch and the Wardrobe* (1950)
	Till We Have Faces: A Myth Untold (1956)
Norman Lindsay	*The Magic Pudding* (1918)
Robert Macfarlane	*Landmarks* (2014)
Sir Thomas Malory	*Le Morte d'Arthur* (1485)
Gabriel García Márquez	*Love in the Time of Cholera* (1985; 1988)
W. Somerset Maugham	*The Moon and Sixpence* (1919)
Daphne du Maurier	*Rebecca* (1938)
Herman Melville	*Moby-Dick* (1851)

Peter Mendelsund	*What We See When We Read* (2014)
John Milton	*Paradise Lost* (1667)
Lucy Maud Montgomery	*Anne of Green Gables* (1908)
Gerald Murnane	*The Plains* (1982)
	Tamarisk Row (1974)
Vladimir Nabokov	*Pale Fire* (1962)
	Lolita (1955)
Edith Nesbit	*The Story of the Treasure Seekers* (1899)
	The Railway Children (1905)
Flann O'Brien	*At Swim-Two-Birds* (1939)
Michael Ondaatje	*Coming Through Slaughter* (1976)
Margaret Paice	*The Secret of Greycliffs* (1961)
Alan Paton	*Cry, the Beloved Country* (1948)
Plato	*Last Days of Socrates*
Eleanor H. Porter	*Pollyanna* (1913)
Marcel Proust	*Remembrance of Things Past* (1913)
Mario Puzo	*The Godfather* (1969)
Arthur Ransome	*Swallows and Amazons* (1930)
Jean Rhys	*Wide Sargasso Sea* (1966)
Henry Handel Richardson	*The Fortunes of Richard Mahony* (1930)
Dr Rumble	*Radio Replies* (1937)
J. D. Salinger	*The Catcher in the Rye* (1951)
	Franny and Zooey (1961)
Walter Scott	*Waverley Novels* (1814–32)
Maurice Sendak	*Where the Wild Things Are* (1963)
Dr Seuss	*The Cat in the Hat* (1957)
	One Fish, Two Fish, Red Fish, Blue Fish (1960)
Anna Sewell	*Black Beauty* (1877)
William Shakespeare	*The Complete Works* (*c.* 1590–1613)
Jane Shaw	*Susan* series (1952–62)
Osbert Sitwell	*Laughter in the Next Room* (1949)
Kenneth Slessor	*Selected Poems* (1944)
Muriel Spark	*The Prime of Miss Jean Brodie* (1961)

Edmund Spenser	*The Faerie Queene* (1590–96)
Johanna Spyri	*Heidi* (1880)
Christina Stead	*The Man Who Loved Children* (1940)
Edward Steichen	*The Family of Man* (1955)
John Steinbeck	*Of Mice and Men* (1937)
Laurence Sterne	*Tristram Shandy* (1759–67)
Robert Louis Stevenson	*Treasure Island* (1881–82)
Rosemary Sutcliff	*The Witch's Brat* (1970)
Alfred, Lord Tennyson	*The Lady of Shalott* (1842)
Hunter S. Thompson	*Fear and Loathing in Las Vegas* (1971)
Morton Thompson	*The Cry and the Covenant* (1949)
J. R. R. Tolkien	*The Hobbit* (1937)
Leo Tolstoy	*Anna Karenina* (1873–77)
John Kennedy Toole	*A Confederacy of Dunces* (1980)
Geoffrey Trease	*Cue for Treason* (1940)
Ethel Turner	*Seven Little Australians* (1894)
Sylvia Townsend Warner	*Absalom, My Son* (1988)
Marian Warren	*No Glamour in Gumboots* (1958)
Nicole Watson	*The Boundary* (2011)
Alan Watts	*The Book: On the Taboo Against Knowing Who You Are* (1966)
Mary Webb	*Precious Bane* (1924)
Helen Wells & Julie Campbell Tatham	*Cherry Ames* series (1943–68)
T. E. White	*The Once and Future King* (1958)
Geoffrey Willans & Ronald Searle	*How to be Topp: a guide to sukcess for tiny pupils, including all there is to kno about SPACE* (1954)
Jeanette Winterson	*The Passion* (1987)
P. G. Wodehouse	*Jeeves* series (1915–74)
Virginia Woolf	*To the Lighthouse* (1927)
Patricia Wrightson	*The Rocks of Honey* (1960)
Johann David Wyss	*The Swiss Family Robinson* (1812)
Lin Yutang	*The Importance of Living* (1937)

Notes on Contributors

Debra Adelaide is the author or editor of more than a dozen books, including the bestselling *Motherlove* series (1996–98) and *Acts of Dog* (2003). Her novels include *The Hotel Albatross* (1995), *Serpent Dust* (1998) and *The Household Guide to Dying* (2008), which was sold around the world. In 2013 she published a collection of short stories, *Letter to George Clooney*. Her new novel is *The Women's Pages* (2015).

Sunil Badami was a reader long before he was a writer, performer and broadcaster. He has written for the *Guardian*, the *Sydney Morning Herald*, *Good Weekend*, the *Australian*, *The Monthly*, the *New Daily*, the *Australian Literary Review*, *Australian Gourmet Traveller*, *Southerly*, *Island* and *Meanjin*, and has been published in Australia and overseas, including in *Best Australian Stories* and *Best Australian Essays*. He recently presented the ABC Local Radio show *Sunday Takeaway* and is currently rewriting his first novel, which he hopes his children will get to read one day.

Gabrielle Carey started writing as a teenager and published her first co-written book, *Puberty Blues*, in 1979. She has since written *In My Father's House*, a biography of her father, *Waiting Room*, a memoir of her mother, and a book of personal essays, *So Many Selves*. Her most recent book, *Moving Among Strangers*, an exploration of her family's connections with the Australian novelist and poet Randolph Stow, was co-winner of the 2014 Prime Minister's Literary Award for Non-Fiction. Carey teaches non-fiction writing at the University of Technology, Sydney.

Luke Davies is the author of three novels (including the cult best-seller *Candy* and more recently *God of Speed*), a children's book, *Magpie*, and six volumes of poetry. His poetry has won the *Age* Book of the Year Prize, the John Bray Poetry Prize at the South Australian Premier's Awards, the Judith Wright Calanthe Poetry Prize at the Queensland Premier's Awards, the Phillip Hodgins Memorial Medal for Poetry, and the Grace Leven Poetry Prize; *Interferon Psalms* won the inaugural Prime Minister's Literary Award for Poetry. He was the co-writer, with Neil Armfield, of the feature film adaptation of *Candy*, starring the late Heath Ledger. His memoir/essay *The Cisco Kid* was nominated for a Southern California Journalism Award with the Los Angeles Press Club. He has featured, as a storyteller, on *This American Life* and *Unfictional*. He is the film critic for *The Monthly*.

Tegan Bennett Daylight is a critic, teacher and fiction writer. She is the author of several books for children and teenagers, the novels *Bombora* (1996), *What Falls Away* (2001) and *Safety* (2006), and has just finished her first collection of short stories, *Six Bedrooms*. Her stories appear in a wide range of Australian journals, including *Griffith Review*, *Meanjin* and *Best Australian Stories*. She lives in the Blue Mountains with her husband and two children.

Delia Falconer is the author of two novels, *The Service of Clouds* and *The Lost Thoughts of Soldiers*, and the memoir *Sydney*. Her fiction and non-fiction have been widely anthologised, including in the *PEN Macquarie Anthology of Australian Literature, The Penguin Century of Australian Stories, Best Australian Essays* and *Best Australian Stories.* She is a senior lecturer in creative writing at the University of Technology, Sydney.

Kate Forsyth is the award-winning and internationally bestselling author of 30 books. She has been voted one of Australia's Favourite 20 Novelists. Her historical novel about the Grimm Brothers, *The Wild Girl*, was named the Most Memorable Love Story of 2013. Her 'Rapunzel' retelling, *Bitter Greens*, received an Honourable Mention in the Norma K. Hemming Award, and was called 'the best fairy-tale retelling since Angela Carter'. Her new book, *The Beast's Garden* (2015) is a retelling of Grimm's *Beauty and the Beast*, set in Nazi Germany. Kate's books for children include *The Impossible Quest, The Gypsy Crown* and *The Puzzle Ring.* An accredited master story-teller, she recently completed a Doctorate of Creative Arts in fairytale retellings. Her website is www.kateforsyth.com.au.

Giulia Giuffrè is a Sydney writer and academic. She has published material on the eighteenth-century novel, biography and auto-biography, caricature, Italian-Australian culture, women's writing and feminism. Her best-known works are *A Writing Life* (1990), *Who Do You Think You Are?* (anthologised in *The Oxford Book of Australian Essays*, ed. Imré Salusinszky, 1997) and her latest book, *Primavera, or The Time of Your Life* (2011). *Primavera* is a memoir of childhood and a compendium of life in general and is now available at primaverathebook.com.

Andy Griffiths is one of Australia's most popular children's authors. Andy is best known for the 'Treehouse' series, the 'JUST!' books and *The Day My Bum Went Psycho.* Over the last twenty years Andy's books have been *New York Times* bestsellers, adapted for the stage and television and won more than fifty Australian children's choice awards. Andy, a passionate advocate for literacy, is an ambassador for the Indigenous Literacy Foundation and the Pyjama Foundation.

Anita Heiss is the author of non-fiction, historical fiction, commercial women's fiction, poetry, social commentary and travel articles. Anita has won four Deadly Awards for Outstanding Achievement in Literature, for her novels *Not Meeting Mr Right*, *Manhattan Dreaming* and *Paris Dreaming* and for the *Macquarie PEN Anthology of Aboriginal Literature.* Anita is an Indigenous Literacy Day ambassador and a proud member of the Wiradjuri nation. Her latest novel is *Tiddas* (2014). Anita calls herself a creative disruptor.

Gail Jones is the author of two short story collections and six novels, the most recent of which are *Five Bells* (2012) and *A Guide to Berlin* (2015). Her fiction has been translated into thirteen languages, has won awards in Australia, and been short-listed for international awards. She has been the recipient of writing fellowships in India, Ireland, Germany, France, the USA and China. She is currently Professor of Writing in the Writing and Society Research Centre at the University of Western Sydney.

Jill Jones has published eight full-length books, including *The Beautiful Anxiety* (2014) and *Ash Is Here, So Are Stars* (2012). She won the 2003 Kenneth Slessor Poetry Prize for *Screens Jets Heaven: New and Selected Poems* (2002) and the 1993 Mary Gilmore Award for *The Mask and the Jagged Star* (1992). Her work has featured in a number of recent anthologies, including the *Macquarie PEN Anthology of Australian Literature* and *The Penguin Anthology of Australian Poetry.* In 2014 she was poet-in-residence at Stockholm University. She is a member of the J. M. Coetzee Centre for Creative Practice, University of Adelaide.

Catherine Keenan is executive director and co-founder of the Sydney Story Factory, a not-for-profit creative-writing centre for young people in Redfern, Sydney. For a decade before that, she was an arts and features writer at the *Sydney Morning Herald*, and also worked as literary editor. She still freelances occasionally for a variety of publications, and is an honorary associate in the Faculty of Education and Social Work at the University of Sydney.

Malcolm Knox has published sixteen books in his own name and ten books in other people's names. He has worked for the *Sydney Morning Herald* since 1994. He has an estimated conversion ratio of eighty books read for one written. His latest novel is *The Wonder Lover* (2015).

Joan London is the author of two prize-winning collections of stories, *Sister Ships*, which won the *Age* Book of the Year in 1986, and *Letter to Constantine*, which won the Steele Rudd Award in 1994 and the Western Australian Premier's Award for Fiction. These stories have been published in one volume as *The New Dark Age*. Her first novel, *Gilgamesh*, was published in 2001, won the *Age* Book of the Year for Fiction in 2002 and was longlisted for the Orange Prize and the International IMPAC Dublin Literary Award. Her second novel, *The Good Parents*, won the 2009 Christina Stead Prize for fiction in the New South Wales Premier's Literary Awards. Her third novel is *The Golden Age* (2014). Joan London's books have all been published internationally to critical acclaim.

Wayne Macauley is a Melbourne writer. He has published four novels, *Blueprints for a Barbed-Wire Canoe*, *Caravan Story*, *The Cook* and *Demons*, and the short fiction collection *Other Stories*. He has been shortlisted for the Victorian and Queensland Premier's Literary Awards, the Western Australian Premier's Book Award and the Melbourne Prize Best Writing Award.

Fiona McFarlane's short stories have been published in *Zoetrope: All-Story*, *Best Australian Stories*, *Southerly* and the *New Yorker*. Her first novel, *The Night Guest*, was shortlisted for the Miles Franklin Award, the Stella Prize, the *LA Times* Book Prize and the Prime Minister's Literary Award. She lives in Sydney.

David Malouf is the internationally acclaimed author of novels including *Ransom*, *The Great World*, *Remembering Babylon*, *An Imaginary Life*, *Conversations at Curlow Creek*, *Dream Stuff*, *Every Move You Make* and his autobiographical classic *12 Edmonstone Street*. Three collections of his writing, *A First Place*, *The Writing Life* and *Being There* are published by Knopf. He was born in 1934 in Brisbane and now lives in Sydney.

Rosie Scott is an internationally published, award-winning author of six novels, a collection each of short stories, poems and essays, and editor of two anthologies. Her play *Say Thank You to the Lady* won the Bruce Mason Playwriting Award in New Zealand, and the movie *Redheads*, which was based on it, won five international awards. She is a permanent member of the Council of the Australian Society of Authors, has received the Sydney PEN Award, was awarded an honorary membership of PEN and in 2004 was nominated with Tom Keneally for the Human Rights Medal. In 2012 she was nominated for the *Sydney Morning Herald*'s *Sydney Magazine*'s 100 most influential people in Sydney for her work in mentoring and teaching about asylum seekers. Her last novel, *Faith Singer*, was selected for the 2004 Orange Prize for Fiction's 50 Essential Reads by Contemporary Writers. Her latest book is *A Country Too Far*, the anthology on asylum seekers, co-edited with Tom Keneally. 'Reading for Life' is an extract from her memoir, *Writing a Revolution*.

Carrie Tiffany was born in West Yorkshire and grew up in Western Australia. She spent her early twenties working as a park ranger in Central Australia and now lives in Melbourne, where she works as an agricultural journalist. Her first novel, *Everyman's Rules for Scientific*

Living, was published in the UK, US, Germany, the Netherlands and Australia. In 2006 it was short-listed for the Miles Franklin Literary Award, the Victorian Premier's Literary Award, the Orange Prize for Fiction, the Commonwealth Writer's Prize and the Guardian First Book Award, and was the winner of the Western Australian Premier's Fiction Prize and the Dobbie Award. Her second novel, *Mateship with Birds*, was long-listed for the Women's Prize for Fiction (UK) and the Miles Franklin Literary Award and short-listed for the Victorian Premier's Literary Award, the Melbourne Prize for Fiction and the Kibble Award. In 2013 *Mateship with Birds* was the winner of the Christina Stead Prize for Fiction and the inaugural Stella Prize.

Geordie Williamson has been chief literary critic of the *Australian* since 2008. In 2011, he was awarded the Pascall Prize for critical writing and the following year he published *The Burning Library*, a collection of essays on neglected figures in Australian literature. His second book is *Lairds of Rapa Nui*, an account of his Scottish family's half-century of sovereignty over Easter Island (2015). He lives in the Blue Mountains with his family.

The Sydney Story Factory

The Sydney Story Factory is a non-profit creative writing centre based at The Martian Embassy and Gift Shop in 176 Redfern Street, Redfern, Sydney. It was founded by Catherine Keenan and Tim Dick and opened in 2012.

A team of volunteer tutors helps young people to write stories of all kinds, which are then published in a variety of ways. Programs target marginalised young people, and those from Indigenous and non-English-speaking backgrounds, but are open to everyone.

The inspiration for the Sydney Story Factory came from 826 Valencia, a writing centre for young people founded by novelist Dave Eggers and educator Ninive Caligari in San Francisco in 2002.

The Simple Act of Reading supports the work of the Sydney Story Factory by donating all profits from the book to encourage reading as well as writing and creativity. Several authors who are supporters of the Sydney Story Factory have contributed to this book.

www.sydneystoryfactory.org.au

Sydney Story FACTORY

Acknowledgements

THIS PROJECT BECAME POSSIBLE DUE TO THE ASSISTANCE of the Copyright Agency's Cultural Fund; everyone involved is grateful for its support for authors.

And the project only turned into a book thanks to the generosity and enthusiasm of the team at Random House. In particular I am indebted to Meredith Curnow, whose expertise and wonderful equanimity have made this entire project a joy to deliver. My thanks also to Catherine Keenan from the Sydney Story Factory, who warmly embraced this idea and gave me valuable support all the way through.

Sincere thanks to all the authors who contributed these essays, and also to those who generously donated their fees back to assist even further the work of the Sydney Story Factory.

Thanks to several authors and publishers for permission to reprint their pieces. Tegan Bennett Daylight's 'A Phone Call to Helen Garner' was first published in the *Australian* (3 November 2012); Luke Davies' 'Hergé and Me' was first published in the *Sydney Morning Herald* (3–4 December 2011); Giulia Giuffrè's 'Reading and Secrets' is an edited version of a chapter from *Primavera or, The Time of Your life* (GAG Publications, 2011); Gail Jones's 'Eleanor Reads Emma' first appeared in her collection *Fetish Lives* (Fremantle Arts Centre Press, 1997); Joan London's 'The Only Russian in Sydney' and Wayne Macauley's 'Far Enough' both first appeared as introductions to the Text Classics' 2012 reprints of *The Watch Tower* and *The Plains* respectively; David Malouf's 'Reading the Signs' was first published in *Jane Eyre* (Oxford Classics, 1998) and reprinted in his collection *The Writing Life* (Knopf, 2014); an earlier version of Carrie Tiffany's 'Wessex' appeared in the *Age* (22 January 2006).